ORDINARY THEOLOG

FAITHFUL

A THEOLOGY OF
SEX

BETH FELKER JONES

GENE L. GREEN, SERIES EDITOR

ZONDERVAN

Faithful
Copyright © 2015 by Beth Felker Jones

This title is also available as a Zondervan ebook. Visit www.zondervan.com/ebooks.

Requests for information should be addressed to:
Zondervan, 3900 Sparks Dr. SE, Grand Rapids, Michigan 49546

Library of Congress Cataloging-in-Publication Data

Jones, Beth Felker, 1976–
     Faithful : a theology of sex / Beth Felker Jones.
        pages cm.—(Ordinary theology)
     Includes bibliographical references.
     ISBN 978-0-310-51827-3 (softcover)
  1. Sex—Religious aspects—Christianity. I. Title.
  BT708.J65 2015
  233'.5—dc23   2014046213

All Scripture quotations, unless otherwise indicated, are from the *New Revised Standard Version of the Bible,* copyright © 1989, Division of Christian Education of the National Council Churches of Christ in the United States of America and are used by permission. All rights reserved.

Any Internet addresses (websites, blogs, etc.) and telephone numbers in this book are offered as a resource. They are not intended in any way to be or imply an endorsement by Zondervan, nor does Zondervan vouch for the content of these sites and numbers for the life of this book.

Cover design: Mikah Kandros
Interior illustration: Beth Shagene
Interior design: Beth Shagene

Printed in the United States of America

HB 02.20.2024

CONTENTS

For my parents, Jo and Dean,
and Brian's parents, Luanne and Rex,
who have embodied faithfulness and so
shown us the love of Christ

FOREWORD TO THE ORDINARY THEOLOGY SERIES

GENE L. GREEN

ORDINARY THEOLOGY. THESE TWO WORDS TOGETHER SOUND like an oxymoron. We're accustomed to thinking about "theology" as the stiff and stifling stuff found in ponderous tomes written by Christian scholars in ivory towers, places far removed from our ordinary lives. We live on the street, in our homes, in places of business, in schools, in gyms, and in churches. What does theology have to do with the ordinary affairs of our daily lives?

We want to bring the Bible into our lives, to be sure, and we attend church to learn about God's Word. We read our favorite passages and wonder how ancient stories about Noah on the water or Jesus on the water relate to the checkout at the grocery store, the hours at work, the novel we read for pleasure, the sicknesses we endure, the votes we cast, or the bed on which we lie. How do we construct a bridge between the biblical worlds and the twenty-first-century world as we seek to follow Jesus faithfully? The distance between our local shopping center and Paul's forum in Athens (Acts 17) seems like an unbridgeable canyon. What does the Bible have to do with the wonderful or difficult realities we face on the baseball field or in the city? How do we receive God's Word, which is truly for all people, at all times, in all places?

It's an old question, one the church has been asking for centuries. The Bible is a historical document with contemporary relevance. But we're also aware that it doesn't seem to speak directly to many situations we face. There is no obvious biblical view of nuclear war, a kind of destruction unknown in the ancient world. What about epidemics such as AIDS, an unknown disease in the ancient world? The Noah story describes a dramatic climate change, but does that cataclysm have anything to do with global warming today? Through the centuries Christians have understood that the Bible cannot be simply proof-texted in all life's situations. Yet we still believe that the Bible is God's Word for us in our complex world. Enter theology.

The word *theology* comes from a couple of Greek terms: *theos* and *logos*. *Theos* means "God" and *logos* means "word." Simply stated, theology is words that express thoughts about God. We hold beliefs about God such as "God is love" (1 John 4:8). We understand that Jesus died for our sins and that we have a hope that transcends the grave because of the resurrection of Christ. All these are theological statements. We have received Christian theology through our parents, church, and Scripture reading, and we attempt to discover how biblically based belief relates to our lives. We do theology as we take Scripture and our inherited theology and seek to work out what God is saying about the issues of today. Every Christian is a theologian.

Ordinary theology is really just another way to say *theology*. The expression emphasizes how theology is part of the ordinary stuff of daily life. Food is a theological topic. We can think about buying food, the need for food, those without food, selling food. What does the Bible have to say about food supply, hunger, and generosity? To ask that question is to think theologically about food. What about government welfare or foreign aid? We can think through the whole of Scripture and apply its perspectives and teachings to such issues. This is theology. And it is something every Christian can and must do. We believe that the gospel is relevant not only to our inner life, but to life in the world. The road we travel as ordinary Christians is to do "ordinary theology" as we work God's message into all aspects of daily life.

The Ordinary Theology Series has a few goals. The first is to take up the common issues of daily life and think through them theologically. But another purpose of the series is to invite you to develop your skills as a theologian. These small books are examples of theological method but also a welcome into the necessary, challenging, and joyous task of doing theology. We're all called to follow the example of the first great Christian theologian whose day job was netting fish for a living. Peter did not receive training in the rabbinic schools as had Paul, yet he was the one who first understood and stated that Jesus was the Christ, the Son of the Living God (Matt. 16:16). He also opened the door of faith to the Gentiles as he came to understand that God accepts every person, regardless of ethnicity (Acts 10). Each of us can make a theological contribution to the church, our family, our community, and our own life. For your sake and the sake of others, be a theologian.

One final word about format. Each chapter begins with a story, and theological reflection follows. Theology happens in the place where Scripture meets us on the road where "life is lived tensely, where thought has its birth in conflict and concern, where choices are made and decisions are carried out."[1] We go to Scripture and the deep well of Christian theology as we develop our theology in

the place where we find ourselves. God is concerned about people
and places and does not ask us to divorce ourselves from them as
we follow and serve Christ. And he gives us guidance on how to
do that. So, enjoy the read! And again: be the theologian.

INTRODUCTION

I NEVER INTENDED TO BE SOMEONE WHO TALKS ABOUT SEX IN public, but the subject fits together with topics I've cared about for a long time: what place bodies have in the Christian faith and how it is that God intends us to thrive as men and women. I'm willing to talk about sex because I think about my work as a theologian as work done in and with and for the church, and the people of God need to be able to think well — and Christianly — about sex.

Sex is a topic that matters. It's personal. It's about our day-to-day lives, about our bodies, about what we want and how we arrange our lives and how we relate to other people.

Strange ideas about sex — odd ideas out of sync with those of the wider culture — marked Christians out from the very beginning. The Scriptures of the Old and New Testaments speak to us about how our bodies honor God. The Bible speaks frankly about sex.

There's no doubt that sexual ethics are important to Christian faith, but what if much in the way Christians teach about sex has gone wrong?

What if, in our efforts to keep young people from making

mistakes, we've done a great deal of damage? What if sex is not about a list of rules, a set of dos and don'ts? What if sex isn't, most of all, about us?

What if sex is about God and who God is and about God's good intentions for creation?

I hope this book might serve as an antidote to some of the poison that has seeped into Christian sexual morality. This isn't a purity book, one that feeds fantasies that we — and especially girls and women — are valuable because we maintain our bodies as some kind of precious vessel or glistening prize. This isn't a book that claims Christians have the best sex ever, one that promises that our reward for following the rules will be mind-blowing sex. This isn't a lay-out-the-rules book, one that claims to get every-thing right by prescribing a perfect path and ignores the ways that none of us are perfect. If you're feeling weary of those kinds of books, I'm with you.

In this book I talk about what sex has to do with God. I try to show that the way Christians do and don't have sex is about who God is and the good life God wants for us. Chapter 1 starts with the idea that sex matters because it is part of a reality that God created and loves. The second chapter explores the Christian idea that all of God's creation — including sex — is good because God is good, and the third chapter acknowledges that much has gone wrong with this good creation. Under the condition of sin, we take what God made good and we twist it and use it for disor-dered purposes. Chapter 4 begins with the good news that God is redeeming creation and that sex doesn't have to stay in the realm of sin. Sex is, by God's power, made holy and loving and good once more. In chapter 5 I draw an analogy between faithful sex and God's faithfulness, and in chapter 6 I talk about the freedom God gives us to make faithful sex possible. Chapter 7 critiques some of the ways Christians have grown accustomed to talking about sex, and the last chapter is a call for Christians to bear witness — with our bodies — to God who is good and loving and faithful.

There's not enough space in this little book to address every aspect of sex, but there is room to place sex within the grand story of what God is up to in the world. I hope that putting sex into this story — the most important and cosmic and personal story of all — will help the church think about what it means that "the body is meant not for fornication but for the Lord" (1 Cor. 6:13). I hope it helps us to think about how we can bear witness to the goodness of God through holy sexuality.

1

SEX AND REALITY

IN MARGARET ATWOOD'S NOVEL *ORYX AND CRAKE*, SHE CRE-
ates a horrific world, a dystopia. Lots of things have gone wrong,
but sex is one area in which brokenness shows up powerfully. The
main character, Jimmy, is in love with a woman named Oryx.
Oryx has an unspeakable past, one of abuse and exploitation, in
which she was cruelly used by child pornographers. Jimmy wants
to know exactly what happened, and he keeps pressing Oryx for
details.

Jimmy asks, "It wasn't real sex, was it? ... In the movies, it was
only acting. Wasn't it?"

Oryx shuts him down with her answer. "But Jimmy, you
should know. All sex is real."[2]

I believe this insight is exactly right: "All sex is real."

Much of what goes wrong around Christian understandings
of sex has to do with our failure to connect sex to reality. We fail
to see that the way we do — and do not — have sex has to do with
who God *really* is and who we *really* are.

When theologians use a word like *real*, we mean serious business. What is most real is God, and whatever it really means to be
human has to do with who God is and with God's good intentions
for us.

Irenaeus, a teacher and leader in the early church, talked

about reality in just this way. Humans, Irenaeus insisted, were not put here to fade away into nothing. This is because God made us and has plans for us. We have a purpose. Since we "are real," Irenaeus writes, we "must have a real existence, not passing away into things which are not, but advancing [to a new stage] among things that are." Irenaeus expects that we will continue to grow, to mature, and to become more and more — really — the human beings that God created us to be.

The idea that "sex is real" is difficult to understand in our world, a world in which a lot of people have something at stake in pretending that sex doesn't *really* matter.

It may help to consider an analogy. Imagine a child who is taught that something is no big deal when, in reality, that something matters deeply. We can use the example of food. Day in and day out, the child hears lines from the following script:

"It doesn't matter what you eat or don't eat."

"Eating has nothing to do with your health."

"Food is just for the body, and what really matters is your psychological health. Bodies and eating have nothing to do with that."

"Food is a private matter."

"If you have a taste for something, you should eat it. Lots of it."

"Whatever you eat in the privacy of your house is your decision. It doesn't affect anyone else."

"Don't ask where your food comes from."

"Nobody gets hurt in the production of your food."

"Nothing you eat can hurt you."

"Nothing you eat will help you to grow strong."

"You might like broccoli, but that doesn't make it good for me. That's just your personal preference."

"Food should always make you happy. Pleasure is the only reason for eating."

Even though the script is detached from reality, the child internalizes it. The child believes it, and the child eats a steady diet of gummy candies and fries. The child has no way to understand the relationship between her diet and the fact that she is not thriving. The child has no way to imagine the relationship between food and reality. While you and I know that food is real, this child lives in a world of lies.

In our cultural moment, it's interesting that we're willing to talk — a lot — about how food matters, but we have no tools for connecting sex to reality. Christians have a long history of recognizing the connections between food and sex. Both food and sex are central, pressing aspects of what it means to be embodied. As embodied creatures, we can't ignore either.

The world we live in tells lies about sex that are analogous to the lies about food above. We're told that it doesn't matter what we do with our bodies. Our world treats bodies as expendable or as mere means to more important ends. If we can be convinced that sex is not "real," that sex doesn't have meaning, that our bodies don't matter, then we will be vulnerable to use and abuse.

If our bodies don't *really* mean anything, then we will act as though we can assign them meaning at random. We will act, or others will want us to act, as though our bodies — free of real meaning — can be used, in a given moment, for nothing but pleasure or nothing but power or nothing but selfishness. We will act as though bodies can be disregarded or discounted. We will act as though bodies can be used as commodities, bought and sold on the free market.

But if sex is real, if bodies matter, then we are accountable to something beyond ourselves, something beyond whatever is in fashion or whatever the market will bear. We are accountable to reality. To truth and goodness and beauty.

We can be set free to imagine that our bodies mean something about who God really is and about the kind of good life — rich and abundant and real — that God wants for us as his beloved children. In the Christian faith, we have resources in Scripture and in Christian teaching to help us think about what sex has to do with reality. We need to claim those resources.

It's common to hear a critique of Christian sexual ethics that goes something like this:

"Why are Christians so hung up on sex anyway? Shouldn't they care more about other problems? Why do Christians act like sexual sin is the one thing we have to take seriously?"

Such critics often go on to dismiss Christian teaching about sexual behavior. These critics claim that Christians are hung up on a bunch of rules that don't actually matter (notice how this criticism makes a claim about reality). Maybe those rules are legalistic hang-ups, the baggage of immature or uptight people who are failing to remember that salvation comes by grace and not from following a set of rules. Worse, critics suggest that those rules come from somewhere devious and twisted — maybe they are about self-righteousness, from people who like to look down on others and condemn what they are doing — maybe they come from hang-ups about the body, from "Puritanical" people who have no room for joy or pleasure in their lives.

I hope that Christian resources that help us understand how "sex is real" will also help us respond to these criticisms. Christian sexual ethics have everything to do with who God is and with what it means to be human.

The critics are right that sexual ethics is not the only area that Christians ought care about, but they are wrong that sex does not matter. Sex matters because it is real. Sex is not incidental, something that we shake off as though it doesn't really touch the core of our existence. Paul, writing to the church in Corinth, names sexual sin four times in a list of ten types of sin (1 Cor. 6:9 – 10). He takes sexual sin seriously because it is so intimate, so personal, and so bodily. Other sins are "outside the body; but the fornicator sins against the body itself" (v. 18). These are not the words of a prude or of someone who has a problem with bodies. These are the words of someone who understands that our bodies are real and that what happens in the body is intimate and personal. Sex matters because embodiment goes to the very heart of what it means to be human.

Scripture teaches in many different ways that sex really matters. The way Christians do — and don't — have sex is anchored in the deepest truth about reality, and it witnesses to the reality of a God who loves and is faithful to his people. More than that, Christian sexual ethics reflect reality because they make sense of the kind of creatures God made us to be, and so those sexual ethics offer us a way to really flourish as human beings. They point to a way to be in relationship with God and with each other that bears faithful witness to the God who *is* love (1 John 4:8), who *is* the truth about reality.

Some contemporary Christians seem to have given up on sexual morality. They assume that it's unrealistic to expect Christians to look different from the world, or they dismiss tradition as outdated. Other Christians accept traditional sexual ethics — not having sex outside of marriage — as a given and assume that there is such a thing as good sexual behavior and bad sexual behavior.

In both cases Christians often have very little idea *why* sex might matter. Whether sexual morality is rejected or is clung to as a norm, many Christians don't have much to say about why sex matters for the Christian life. Even where we accept classic Christian teaching about sex, we still may have trouble acting on those beliefs. Most of us don't know how to explain Christian teaching on sex to people who are not Christians, people who might be put off from Christianity by its strange sexual ethics.

I hope this book addresses this by talking about sex in a way that shows how Christian sexuality is not a series of legalistic morals but is instead meant to be a witness to the God who is faithful to Israel and to us. Sex matters to God because bodies matter to God, because God created our bodies and has good plans for us as embodied people. Sex is a witness to what God does in our lives, the same God who says to Israel, "I will take you for my wife forever; I will take you for my wife in righteousness and in justice, in steadfast love, and in mercy. I will take you for my wife in faithfulness; and you shall know the LORD" (Hos. 2:19–20).

The early church assumed that sex is real, that it matters. We see one important example of this in Acts 15. This is a record of a defining moment for the people of God. The Christian church — which had been up to that point mostly a Jewish church — was figuring out how to open itself up to people who were not Jews.

The church was feeling its way forward as it tried to understand what it means to be a people of many nations. Questions circled around obedience to the law as revealed in the Old Testament. Would new Gentile believers be bound to the full weight of the Jewish law? Specifically, would they need to be circumcised when they converted to Christianity? We can imagine this question felt very, very real to the new Gentile convert whose genitals were being discussed.

These early Christians made a crucial decision. New Christians would *not* be bound to the law. They would have freedom in Christ to come into the people of God without having to be circumcised, without having the mark of God's covenant with Israel on their bodies. This decision was extremely significant, and it only makes sense if Paul is right when he teaches that "in Christ Jesus neither circumcision nor uncircumcision counts for anything; the only thing that counts is faith working through love" (Gal. 5:6).

The church knew this, knew that "for freedom Christ has set us free" (Gal. 5:1). When we read Acts 15, we read about the very good news that is ours in Jesus Christ. God cleanses our hearts by faith (v. 9). As circumcision marks the Jews as God's people, Christians are marked by baptism, shared by all believers. We belong to God, not because of anything we have done — not because of circumcision and not because of sexual morality — but because of what Christ has done for us. This is central to the gospel, central to Christian faith. There is real goodness and truth and beauty here.

Right now, my imaginary critic — the one who thinks Christian sexual morality is nothing but legalism — might think their argument has been clinched. After all, the early church refused to bind Gentile Christians to legal obedience, so surely traditional and biblical restrictions on Christian sexual behavior should be thrown out. If we keep reading in the book of Acts, however, we find a different set of expectations.

Gentile converts will not have to be circumcised, but they *are* absolutely expected to live their lives in a way that witnesses to who God is and to what Christ has done. They will not have to be circumcised, but they *will* have their lives changed by the gospel.

They will not have to be circumcised, but their bodies will be signs of what God has done.

Gentile believers are not bound by the full weight of the ceremonial law, but all believers are still expected to live according to the "essentials" (v. 28). It is significant that these essentials, as named here in Acts, are only two. The first is an anti-idolatry command; don't eat meat sacrificed to idols. The second is to "abstain" from "fornication" (v. 29).

Right here, in the middle of the gospel recognition that we are free in Christ, sexual ethics are reaffirmed and cemented as essential to the Christian life. Here, in recognizing that Christians will have a new relationship to the law, the church also recognized that sexual ethics matter.

As the apostles are in the middle of the "joy" (v. 3) of seeing lives changed by the grace of Jesus Christ, they ask God's people to avoid fornication. It seems clear that sexual ethics are not just legalism. They are, somehow, "essential." Sexual ethics are part of the way that God changes our lives, helping us to become more and more like Jesus and to be more faithful in bearing God's image in the world. Sexual ethics are essential because faithful sex testifies to the power and the character of the God who saves. Sex is very real.

2

CREATED GOODNESS

A FRIEND TOLD ME A STORY ABOUT HER GRANDMOTHER. During time spent in a nursing home, her grandma was abused. When the family discovered the abuse, there was a financial settlement. My friend, naturally, found this situation upsetting, and she mentioned to her mom that she wished the whole thing had never happened. Her mom was more cavalier. She responded that she thought the situation was a "win-win."

As her mother saw it, nothing that happened to grandma's body *mattered* — it wouldn't be part of her life in heaven — and the family got significant settlement money from the situation. But bodies do matter. The Scriptures don't point us toward a disembodied heaven. They promise the hope of future resurrection, of "a new heaven and a new earth" (Rev. 21:1), and they assure us that we matter — body and soul — to God. Bodies are real, and my friend was right to be horrified, not only by what her grandmother suffered, but also by her mother's response.

I don't think the mom in this story was trying to be cold, but she'd probably received some bad teaching about where Christianity stands on questions about the body. Christians can never think of the body as something that doesn't matter. Bodies are God's good creations, and resurrection bodies are included in

God's good final plans for his everlasting kingdom. Grandma's body, in this life and in the next, is precious to God.

The Christian faith is profoundly *for* the body and *for* the joys of the bodily life. God, after all, created us — body and soul — and called creation good. Furthermore, God is redeeming us — body and soul — so that we may "bear the image of the man of heaven" (1 Cor. 15:49) and show the love of God to a world in need.

Being *for* the body means that what we do, in the body, matters. According to Paul, we're the people who are "always carrying in the body the death of Jesus, so that the life of Jesus may also be made visible in our bodies" (2 Cor. 4:10). The life of Jesus is supposed to be visible in our flesh. People who see us should be able to see the gospel of Jesus Christ. Given this, it shouldn't surprise us that the life of the body — including things like eating and sex — matters.

Christians have to recognize that bodies matter because of what we believe about creation and about God, who is the Creator. One of the most Christian things we can do is to affirm the goodness of creation. We know that creation is good, and we are meant to act on the truth that creation is good. This was a distinctly Christian move — a counter cultural move — in the days of the early church. This same insistence is a distinctly Christian, countercultural move in our time.

In the early days of Christianity, the threat to creation's goodness came in the form of a heresy called Gnosticism. Gnostics denied the goodness of creation. If we study Gnostic groups that were active in the early centuries of the church, we find that quite a collection of them existed. They weren't all exactly the same, but they shared certain key teachings, teachings that Christian faith recognized as false.

What key features did those Gnostic groups share? First, they were insider groups. That is, they divided the world into two groups: those in-the-know and those who didn't have their special in-group knowledge. Gnosticism was thus, by nature, elitist. The secret in-group knowledge (the *gnosis* that gives the Gnostics their name) wasn't for just anybody. It was only for those who were in the Gnostic fold, and that left those on the outside in a sad position, because the Gnostics believed that their salvation came through that insider knowledge.

For our purposes here, the second key feature shared by ancient Gnostic groups is even more important and more problematic than their belief in secret knowledge. That second feature denied the goodness of material creation. Gnosticism divided the world in two: material and spiritual. And it taught that one part is good and one part is bad. We can call this feature of Gnostic thought "hierarchical dualism." It's a "dualism" because it divides everything in two.

Material and spiritual.

Body and soul.

It's "hierarchical" because it teaches that one of those two parts is superior. It's not just that the material world and the spiritual world exist. For Gnostics, they exist in opposition to each other.

Material against spiritual.

Body against soul.

In a Gnostic worldview, the material world — including bodies and sex — is something nasty, degraded.

All this was intertwined with Gnostic beliefs about who God is and what God creates. Because Gnostics disdained the material world — disdained stuff, and bodies, and dirt — they couldn't believe that God created that world. Instead, they taught that the existence of the material world was a problem. Maybe a lesser being, a demigod or some cosmic trickster, had created that material world. Maybe the material world existed as a punishment.

Gnostic hierarchical dualism went hand in hand with Gnostic sexual ethics and sexual practice. Peter Brown digs into the historical nitty-gritty of Gnosticism to show us an understanding of sexual desire "as an enduring feature of the unredeemed human person.... Sex was 'the unclean rubbing that is from the fearful fire that came from the fleshly part.'" For the Gnostic, flesh is bad and sex is impure. Simply to be a sexual person is to be unredeemed.

While this goes against Christian teaching about the goodness of creation, the goodness of the body, and the goodness of sex as a gift from God, it's easy to see that a Gnostic type understanding has — in many times and places — infected Christianity. Christians, like the Gnostics, have sometimes had a hard time imagining what it could mean to be both sexual and redeemed. Embracing the goodness of creation and God's good purposes for embodied life will require that we fight against those Gnostic impulses.

All of this gets very personal. It influences what we do, and it touches our bodies. The mistaken judgment that sex is bad is connected to abuses. Kurt Rudolph links the ancient Gnostic "rejection of creation" with rejecting "conventional conceptions of morality. Two contrary and extreme conclusions could be drawn: the libertine ... and the ascetic."[5]

The "libertine" concludes that, because bodies don't matter, we can do whatever we want with them. The claim is that we can do whatever we want with the body — and whatever we want sexually — because sex and bodies don't *really* mean anything. Here, discounting bodies and sex leads to reckless indulgence, to the erasing of boundaries. Libertine Gnosticism is there in our hook-up culture, a culture that denies that bodies matter, discourages authentic relationships, and tries to turn sex into a hobby or a low-value biological need.

The "ascetic" concludes that, because bodies are a problem, we should deny and denigrate them. This kind of Gnostic asceticism cannot see the body's goodness and will take disciplining the body to punishing extremes. Here, discounting bodies and sex leads to a rejection of the goods of creation, and it plays out in a superstrict ethic that leaves no room for healthy, happy sexuality. Ascetic Gnosticism is there in the marriage where someone feels guilty about enjoying sex. It's there in the hatred of the body that deprives it of calories and subjects it to punishing exercise, and it's there when we stand in front of the mirror and hate our thighs, hate our stomachs, hate our chins.

The New Testament suggests that both the libertine and the ascetic misuses of sex tempted some early Christians, and it's interesting that both temptations seem to have existed in the same church setting — Corinth. Those on the libertine end of the spectrum allowed for gluttony and excess and promiscuous sex. They said things like "Let us eat and drink, for tomorrow we die" (1 Cor. 15:32) or "All things are lawful for me" or "Food is meant for the stomach and the stomach for food"(1 Cor. 6:12 – 13). All these statements discount the importance — the reality — of the body and the bodily life.

Paul counters these libertine slogans with reminders of the bodily resurrection (1 Cor. 15). He also counsels believers that "not all things are beneficial" (1 Cor. 6:12) and that the body is "for the Lord" (v. 13). Because Christ has been raised from the dead, in the body, bodies matter. Because God has good purposes for us, bodies matter.

Christians who advocated an extreme ascetic position wanted to deny or even punish the life of the body. Practical outcomes of this position include taking fasting to dangerous extremes or claiming that Christians should never marry or have sex. In Corinth, Paul had to address this among those who said, "It is well for a man not to touch a woman" (1 Cor. 7:1).

Maybe these ascetic rigorists thought Paul would be on their side since he was unmarried, but he corrects them just as he corrected the libertines. Paul offers clear counsel; married folk should have sex and should not "deprive one another" (v. 5). Against a body-denying, creation-denying ethic of sexual renunciation, Paul clarifies that marriage — and, even more, sex in marriage — is not a sin (v. 36).

Paul teaches that sex is a good gift from God. Though he is certainly aware of the ways that sex can go wrong, he refuses the false solution of extreme asceticism. The fact that something can be abused, as in "cases of sexual immorality" (v. 2), is no reason to deny its goodness. When we read 1 Corinthians together with 1 Timothy, the logic against extreme asceticism becomes even clearer. Against those who "forbid marriage and demand abstinence from foods" (1 Tim. 4:3), Paul insists that "everything created by God is good, and nothing is to be rejected, provided it is received with thanksgiving" (v. 4).

The Gnostic idea that the body is evil denies the truth about God revealed in Scripture and is a serious threat to the life of Christian discipleship. Gnosticism threatens the way Christians are supposed to *be* in the world. Where the Gnostics taught that creation is divided in two and that materiality is a nasty problem, the early church insisted on the goodness of the *whole* of creation — spiritual and material, seen and unseen. Jesus is the one for whom "all things in heaven and on earth were created, things visible and invisible, whether thrones or dominions or rulers or powers — all things have been created through him and for him" (Col. 1:16). Jesus is truly the savior "of the world" (John 4:42).

Not against the world. Not away from the world. Jesus is for the world.

And that means Jesus is for sex (that is, in favor of it), and sex is for Jesus (as in the verse from Colossians quoted just above).

Why do Christians recognize the whole world — including bodies, including physicality, including sexuality — as good? The answer is theological, that is, it has to do with who God is. Because God, who is good, made all that is, all that is reflects the goodness of God. Because God, who is good, created everything — material and spiritual, bodies and souls, apes and angels — everything belongs to that good God.

Everything is God's work, the "heavens and the earth" (Gen. 1:1). The first chapter of Genesis testifies to God as the creator of everything. God created the whole, the totality, and God is specific in calling all that everything "good." Waters and land are good. Plants and animals are good. Human beings, made in God's own image, are good. "God saw everything that he had made, and indeed, it was very good" (v. 31).

Like the word *real*, when theologians use a word like *good*, we mean business. This isn't a weak little word, one that doesn't point to anything real. This is a word that refers — first and properly — to God.

Jesus uses the word good in this way too, when, "as he was setting out on a journey, a man ran up and knelt before him, and asked him, 'Good Teacher, what must I do to inherit eternal life?'" (Mark 10:17). Jesus seizes on that word — *good* — and says, "Why do you call me good? No one is good but God alone" (v. 18).

Part of the fun of this passage of Scripture is that Jesus *is* God, really. Perhaps the man who came to him, asking for eternal life, recognized this on some level. Only the true God, in goodness, can offer eternal life. If Jesus were anything less than God who is good, then it would make no sense for the man to come to him seeking salvation. In any case, we can recognize the theological heft here. God is good.

When we recognize that creation is also good, we're again saying something theological. We're saying that creation has something to do with who God is. We're saying something with solemn weight. We're talking — as in the first chapter of this book — about reality. The goodness of creation is part of the deepest truth about reality. The goodness of creation is real because the good God is real.

The first chapter of Genesis teaches us about created goodness, and that chapter also contributes to a theological vision of human relationship and of sex. The very existence of human relationship is good. Embodied difference is good. Sex, marriage, and fruitfulness are all God's good creation. Here, in the same place that we learn about created goodness, we learn that God made human beings in God's own image (Gen. 1:26 – 27), and that God made us — these creatures who bear his image — "male and female" (v. 27).

God gave us good work to do, and the goodness of that is part of the goodness of creation. Two words, in Genesis, point to the richness and the character of this work. Human beings are to exercise "dominion" and human beings are to be "fruitful" (v. 28). As creatures made in God's own image, we're supposed to do this work in a way that tells the truth about God. Dominion, then, cannot mean using up the world for our selfish purposes. It must mean stewarding the world in a way that mirrors God's own care for the world in leading it toward the kingdom. Fruitfulness, while it includes the biological fruitfulness of having babies, must also be about the fruit of the Spirit (Gal. 5) who is God and who makes us fruitful.

This good work — dominion and fruitfulness — is given to embodied human beings, human beings who are male and female, human beings who are supposed to witness — to the world at large and to one another — to the goodness of God.

Dominion and fruitfulness are embodied work, and dominion and fruitfulness are, in a certain way at least, work that has to do with sex. Human work is to garden, to be put in "Eden to till it and keep it" (Gen. 2:15). Human work is done in community, and that community includes sexual differentiation — the fact that we are created male and female.

We've heard the word "good" many times in the creation story, and then we encounter a jarring "not good" in Genesis 2:18; "It is not good," says God, "that the man should be alone." That "not good" should startle us. The text has been leading us, so far, on a blissful tour through the garden of delights that is God's creation. The "not good" seems to come out of nowhere, begging us to pay attention to it.

How does it even make sense to say that the man is "alone"? He is — after all — with God. He is in relationship with God, enjoying the sort of intimacy with the Creator that human beings have been missing ever since. Some types of piety might tell him to shut up and be happy. What can he need or want when he walks with God?

But the text testifies otherwise. Of course the man's relationship with God is a central matter. The fact that we're created to be in relationship with God is a key point here, but God's judgment that something is "not good" tells us that we're created for something else too.

We're created to be in relationship with other human beings, in relationship with other embodied creatures who are — like us — not God but who are — like us — created in God's own image.

God, who is beyond all that is created, chose to make us like him when he created us in the divine image. At the same time, God, who is beyond all that is created, is always other than creation. One of the ways that God is other than us is that God, who does not have a body, chose to make human beings embodied. What if at least part of the "not good" of the human creature's aloneness is that there is no other embodied creature who is like him?

God solves the "not good" involved in humans being alone, and God's solution includes embodied difference. God makes another human, and the first human responds with both joy and relief. There is relief that he'll have someone to share his bodily life with besides the animals of the field and the birds of the air (2:19) — relief that he, who is embodied, can be in real relationship with another embodied creature like him. And there is joy over both shared humanity and bodily difference.

Adam sings a little love song: "This at last is bone of my bones and flesh of my flesh; this one shall be called Woman, for out of Man this one was taken" (v. 23).

I'm more and more aware of how hard it is becoming to say that maleness and femaleness are created goods.

In part, this difficulty is born of a real insight. It's the insight of a young man who told my class a story about how he'd taken a survey designed to identify gifts for leadership, how the instrument had identified one of his gifts as "gentleness."

He told us how he reacted with embarrassment. A bit of shame.

Because gentleness isn't manly.

By the grace of God and the power of the Holy Spirit, he immediately reevaluated that reaction. He knew that gentleness is a fruit of the Holy Spirit. He knew that his gentleness was not something to regret but was, instead, a gift from God.

This story haunts me. How many men and women are crippled by stereotyped, sin-laden assumptions about what it means to be "manly" or "womanly"? How many Christians, how many churches, how many marriages are harmed by distorted understandings of what it means to be male and female? How many one-flesh unions are harmed because of sinful ideas about being manly or womanly?

When the man in my story recognized that his culturally ingrained assumptions about what it means to "be a man" couldn't possibly reflect God's good intentions for him, he was recognizing something of huge importance. We need a full and careful acknowledgment of the ways we get gender wrong under the condition of sin.

It's common practice to make a distinction between *sex* and *gender*. The word *sex* is used to refer to the biological reality of bodies, the physical facts of maleness and femaleness, while the word *gender* refers to the social reality of masculinity and femininity. This distinction lines up with conversations about the roles that nature and nurture play in shaping human beings. Nature, here, is the existence of male and female bodies. Nurture is gender, the ways that we learn, through the social world, to act masculine or feminine.

This distinction is helpful in that it points out that many things about the way we go about being male and female are socially constructed. They come, not from our bodies, but from ways that we're shaped by the world. It's important to recognize this because many of these socially constructed ways of being male and female are, in fact, sinful distortions of maleness and femaleness. The vile idea that gentleness isn't masculine or the dangerous idea that grown women shouldn't have body fat are sinful distortions of masculinity and femininity. These distorted ideas aren't what our good God intended for us when he gave us sexually differentiated bodies.

Some social constructions of masculinity and femininity may not be sinful, but it's still a good idea to recognize that they don't come from our bodies, because that recognition keeps us from bullying and marginalizing men and women who don't follow those conventions. For example, I doubt the fact that we assign blue blankets to baby boys and pink ones to baby girls is sinful. Both pink and blue are lovely colors. But the fact that we assign blue to boys and pink to girls is not natural. It's not, in some way, connected to our bodies, and so the social norms of pinkness and blueness can *become* sinful when we use them to cast scorn on people who prefer to wrap their babies in green or to mock a little boy who wants a pink bedspread or to refuse to get a little girl the science set she wants for Christmas because it isn't pink.

To make a distinction between sex and gender, then, can help us, as Christians, to understand the fact that one can be a good son or daughter of God without necessarily conforming to social rules about who wears blue and who wears pink. It can also help us to recognize that growing in holiness as a son or daughter of God sometimes requires defying social rules about men not being gentle or women needing to eat so little that they cannot thrive.

All this is useful. What is less helpful about the distinction between sex and gender, nature and nurture, is that — in practice — the two are often impossible to split apart. The two categories slip into one another, and sometimes that slippage tempts us to give up on maleness and femaleness altogether.

To recognize that things in this fallen world aren't the way they're supposed to be is a basic tenet of Christian faith, but to recognize that we may, in sin, distort something is not the same thing as to deny the reality of that something. Some things about masculinity and femininity are sheer artifice and some things about masculinity and femininity are downright harmful to the beloved children of God.

But that doesn't stop maleness and femaleness from being created goods. Male bodies are good. Female bodies are good. God made them and God loves them.

Whenever humans have denied this, the result has been bad for female bodies, for girls and women. Some ancient Gnostics, for instance, taught that sexed bodies would be erased in our salvation. This might sound like liberation, especially to, for instance, a woman who has been hurt because of being a woman, but if we take a closer look, we see that these Gnostics see female bodies — far more than male ones — as the special problem that redemption needs to get rid of. We find texts that suggest that a woman may be saved by becoming male, and we have records of extreme ascetic practice among women — hard core fasting — being celebrated because it erased the femaleness of their bodies as starvation shrunk breasts and ended menstruation.

To be "saved" by destroying women cannot be and never has been good for women. This is the fundamental reason that I don't buy arguments that would do away with so-called "binary sexuality" — the understanding that humans exist in two sexes, male and female. Scripture teaches that we were created male and female and that God loves us as such. A sinful world may hate and despise female bodies (and lots of other bodies too), but God loves them and plans to redeem them.

Moves to ignore maleness and femaleness as created goods are so often moves to denigrate the female. How can we refuse to do so? How can we witness to the goodness of male bodies, the goodness of female bodies, more clearly? How can we do so in a world that would denigrate male and female bodies?

Part of the answer is that Christians need to emphasize redemption. Maleness and femaleness are created goods, but — more — they are redeemed goods.

We need to treasure male and female bodies as good and as loved by God, and we need to do so without assigning sinful meanings to those bodies. I suspect that the seemingly desperate need some Christians seem to have to say what it means to be a man, what it means to be a woman, is born of a quasi-Gnostic refusal to value bodies as such. What if we just let bodies be enough?

How do we embrace the goodness of our created bodies, embrace the goodness of male bodies and female bodies, without sinking into sad, silly stereotypes that would give those bodies meanings that contradict God's good intentions for us? (Meanings like men must be rough, not gentle, or women must be self-effacing in a way that keeps them from doing powerful work of the Spirit to which God calls us all.)

Historic Christianity has assumed that marriage and sex bring together — united in one flesh — two sexually differentiated bodies. The fact of that difference is part of the beauty of marriage and is a fruitful difference. Reproductive biology, too, is a created good.

As Christians, we recognize that God made us as good, embodied, sexually differentiated creatures. It matters that our embodied goodness — and our image bearing — includes both maleness and femaleness. Being created male and female isn't the only thing that matters about being human, neither is it the most important thing. (That most important thing, most Christians would agree, is being created in God's image.) But maleness and femaleness still matters. It's embodied, and it's God's creative intention for us, and it's good.

God creates the goodness of male bodies, and God creates the goodness of female bodies. When those bodies come together in the one-flesh union of marriage, they are united in delight and in partnership. Because God has made men and women, because he has made both in his image, because he has given us embodied difference, we receive the gift of marriage. Because God creates us male and female, "a man leaves his father and his mother and clings to his wife, and they become one flesh" (Gen. 2:24). Naked, sexually differentiated bodies are God's good gift. Imagine the conditions of creation in which "the man and his wife were both naked, and were not ashamed" (v. 25).

When a group of Pharisees ask Jesus a question about marriage, Jesus quotes Genesis. "From the beginning of creation," Jesus says, "'God made them male and female.' 'For this reason a man shall leave his father and mother and be joined to his wife, and the two shall become one flesh'" (Mark 10:6–8). In quoting Genesis, Jesus invokes God's good, creative intentions for us as male and female. He places marriage and sex within the context of God's purposes for creation

Sex is God's good creation and one of God's good gifts to us as his beloved children. It's not nasty or dirty or a problem. Sex is something we can receive with delight, with gratitude to the One whose good creation it is.

Sex is real, and sex is good.

3

SEX GONE WRONG

JOSEPH GORDON-LEVITT'S 2013 FILM, *DON JON*, OFFERS insight into a bleak world in which pornography reigns. Gordon-Levitt plays the lead role; his friends call him "Don Jon" because of his polished routine of bedding beautiful women. This routine is predictably interrupted by bombshell Barbara, played by Scarlett Johansson. Barbara is not about to fall into bed with Jon. First, she is going to make demands. She is absolute and intentional in withholding and using sex as a tool to shape Jon. She wants him to play the role of the perfect boyfriend.

Where the audience expects Barbara to change Jon's life for the better, *Don Jon* moves into creative territory instead. Instead of delivering the expected story — a porn addict saved by a good woman — we watch the unhealthy collision of two people who are capable only of severely broken relationships. The brokenness of the porn addict crashes against that of the pampered princess, creating even more damage. Jon is captivated by Barbara until she finally gets into his bed. Immediately, he is drawn away from the woman beside him and back into his routine of escape into pornography.

This is a world drenched in digital escape from reality. A world in which Jon's captivity to the porn on his laptop is reinforced, again and again, by the difference between the digital images and real women. This is a world in which Jon searches for just the right clip, where he can sort his escapist preferences by hair color and cup size.

But the real insight of the film is that the bleakness of this world isn't confined to pornography. It's also there in the romance movies Barbara adores, movies that Jon disdains. "I don't watch too many movies," Jon says; "everyone knows it's fake, but they watch it like it's real life."

He seems unaware of how this insight applies to his own porn addiction.

Neither Jon nor Barbara knows how to talk about the reality of sex, and both are drawn into escapist fantasies that keep them from having a healthy relationship — one of intimacy and mutuality, partnership and commitment — with each other.

Don Jon diagnoses epidemic pornography, not as the heart of our problems but as a symptom of something else. Pornography is a symptom of diseased relationship in a world that privileges polished images over human truths, a world in which human bodies are offered up on the altar of consumer capitalism.

On that unholy altar, those bodies are broken, mutilated, and cut off from real relationship with God and with other human beings.

Bodies and sex are good, but we all know that sex can and does go wrong. Sex — in a fallen world — happens in hurtful ways and in ways that fail to tell the good truth about who God is. Sin exploits God's good creation and twists it into something distorted and broken.

In Genesis chapter 3, we see a number of pointers to the ways that sin affects human relationships in general and sex in particular. This short text is rich with implications. It suggests a great deal about what sin does to God's good gifts of relationship, bodies, and sex. We learn from Scripture that these effects of sin are not the way things are supposed to be. The one-flesh union of Eden — marked by commitment and mutuality and partnership and delight — is God's good, creative intention for sex. But we cannot ignore the effects of sin in our world and in our own lives.

As we look again at Genesis, where we first learn about sin and about life in a fallen world, it's remarkable how many of the effects of sin, as called out in this story, are felt in human sexuality, human relationships, and human bodies. When Adam and Eve disobeyed God, "the eyes of both were opened, and they knew that they were naked; and they sewed fig leaves together and made loincloths for themselves" (Gen. 3:7). Life under the condition of sin is that life in which it is no longer possible to be naked and unashamed (Gen. 2:25). Under the reign of sin, we feel shame about our bodies; and Adam and Eve covering their genitals is a sign that that shame is connected to sex. Sin means that human beings want — and sometimes need — to hide from themselves and from one another.

Afraid, the fallen Eve and Adam hide from "the presence of the LORD God" (Gen. 3:8). Shame and hiding disrupt human relationships, but they also interfere in the relationship between human beings and God.

God, though, won't let us stay hidden; "Who told you that you were naked? Have you eaten from the tree of which I commanded you not to eat" (v. 11)? And Adam answers, "The woman whom you gave to be with me, she gave me fruit from the tree, and I ate" (v. 12). God says to Eve, "What is this that you have done?" And Eve replies, "The serpent tricked me, and I ate" (v. 13). Life under the condition of sin is that life in which both men and women refuse to take responsibility for their actions. Above, the man blames his wife, and the woman blames the serpent. Neither one confesses, and neither one takes responsibility for having broken faith with God.

God describes what life will be like for human beings bound by sin:

> To the woman he said, "I will greatly increase your pangs in childbearing; in pain you shall bring forth children, yet your desire shall be for your husband, and he shall rule over you." And to the man he said, "Because you have listened to the voice of your wife, and have eaten of the tree about which I commanded you, 'You shall not eat of it,' cursed is the ground because of you; in toil you shall eat of it all the days of your life; thorns and thistles it shall bring forth for you; and you shall eat the plants of the field. By the sweat of your face you shall eat bread until you return to the ground, for out of it you were taken; you are dust, and to dust you shall return." (Gen. 3:16 – 19)

The consequences of sin are felt in our bodies, in our maleness and our femaleness, and in our work. Sin breaks into the marriage relationship, taking what ought to have been good desire and twisting it into something broken.

But desire itself is not sin, nor is our situation without hope. Theologian Sarah Coakley calls desire "the precious clue that ever tugs at the heart, reminding the human soul — however dimly — of its created source."[6] Coakley writes about "putting desire for God above all other desires" and about "judging human desires only in that light."[7]

As we grow practiced in the Christian life, we learn that desire — properly speaking — is *for* God. God is the One for whom we were created, the One for whom we long. The psalmist compares us to thirsty animals: "As a deer longs for flowing streams, so my soul longs for you, O God. My soul thirsts for

God, for the living God. When shall I come and behold the face of God?" (Ps. 42:1–2).

We're meant to yearn for God. God is the purpose of desire, and surely God created all good things — including sex and marriage — to point us to him. Perhaps the fact that, under the condition of sin, the woman's desire will be for her husband (Gen. 3:16) points to the way we may put another human being — a spouse, a husband — into God's place. Under sin, desire, which ought to be good, is twisted. Humans are made into idols, and we forget that God is the One who satisfies our desires. This isn't some quasi-Gnostic claim that sex and bodies don't matter, as if human desire should somehow detach from human bodies. This is rather a claim that we need to take sex and bodies seriously enough to understand them as part of the work of God.

Sin distorts desire, but it also distorts authority. Thankfully, rule too is properly *for* God. God is "the blessed and only Sovereign, the King of kings and Lord of lords" (1 Tim. 6:15). God is the true ruler of creation, and any human rulers are meant to point us to him. Perhaps the fact that, under the condition of sin, the husband "will rule over" (Gen. 3:16) his wife is indicative of the way that one-flesh unions go wrong when husbands would become dictators who control their wives. Under sin, dominion, which ought to be good, is twisted. Instead of women and men exercising dominion together, as we were made to do (Gen. 1:28), women are denigrated and abused, and husbands fail to love their "wives, just as Christ loved the church and gave himself up for her" (Eph. 5:25).

Perhaps the fact that these consequences of sin are gendered — they affect men and women differently — reveals something of the ways that we get being male and female wrong under the condition of sin. Where we were created to share the good work of dominion and fruitfulness, work under the condition of sin separates men and women, twists both dominion and fruitfulness into parodies of what they were meant to be. It is clear that sin distorts the way we do marriage and sex and the way we live together as male and female.

None of us can escape the grasp of sin, and we've all left the garden behind. But God does not leave us behind. Even under the condition of sin, God is there with us and for us, and he cares for us enough to protect us in a sinful world. It is significant that "the LORD God made garments of skins for the man and for his wife, and clothed them" (Gen. 3:21).

In contemporary North America, it's become very difficult to talk about any kind of sex as bad sex. We live with enormous cultural pressures to tolerate any and all "private" behavior. This pressure makes it difficult for our lives — body and soul — to mean anything. Because we're told that sex is private, that it's "none of our business," we have difficulty recognizing the distortions of sin as the distortions that they are. We're tempted to write them off as private choices.

But if we want to mean something, if we want to show the world — in truth and beauty — what it means to "glorify God" in our bodies (1 Cor. 6:20), we have to be able to see distortion as distortion. We need the tools to discern when sex tells the truth about God and supports human flourishing and when sex denies the reality of God and is harmful to human beings. We must have a way to diagnose the situation we're in, to know when we're not embodying the truth of the God who is faithful. We need to be able to recognize when we're embodying, instead, brokenness and idolatry and sin.

God's good intention is for sex to embody a one-flesh union. That union is supposed to be radical, permanent, and intimate.

It's supposed to be about mutual fidelity and to affirm the goodness of bodies and of sexual difference. In the ancient but still persuasive categories of Augustine — the most influential Christian pastor of all time — sex should embody three "goods." Good sex enables or creates or testifies to or delights in (1) fidelity, (2) fruitfulness, and (3) the relationship of the husband and the wife to God.

Fallen sex is selfish. It cares only about the self. Augustine tells us that good, married sex isn't just about the self. It's *for* others: for the spouse, for the world, and for God. Good sex treasures and tends and builds up the beloved. Good sex attends to the beloved, not just in bed, but in the unified life together where both partners learn to die to self and to serve one another in love.

The good of fruitfulness points sex beyond the two spouses toward those who are the fruit of their sexual union. Good sex is fruitful in that it points us toward kingdom work. The good of fruitfulness means that sex is *for* others. This is true in the profound and embodied sense that sex results in procreation, and good sex points us to our children. But this is also true in the equally profound and embodied sense that marital unions should bear fruit in the world — kingdom fruit — in the good work of both partners. Babies are the fruit of sex, and so is the other good work that comes from one-flesh unions: the writing of books, the washing of feet, the teaching of Sunday school, the feeding of the hungry, the hospitality of the dinner table ...

Good sex points both spouses toward God. Augustine's third good, here, teaches us that sex is *for* God. This is true in the sense that sex should be received as a good gift. It's true in the sense that fidelity and fruitfulness are possible only by the power of God's grace. God provides us with manifold goods — including fidelity and fruitfulness and grace — that order our sexuality away from idols, that turn our sexuality from ingrown selfishness to kingdom work, and that train us to point our whole lives — body and soul, sex included — toward the only One who can truly satisfy the thirsty animals that we are, the God we have met in Jesus Christ who promises that "those who drink of the water that I will give them will never be thirsty. The water that I will give will become in them a spring of water gushing up to eternal life" (John 4:14).

But fallen sex strains against all this goodness, and we know the damaging, distorting reality of sin in the world and in our bodies. Sex and bodies and marriage are good, but God's good gifts can be twisted and distorted. Good sex can — and does — become bad sex. Scripture tells the truth about the reality of sex gone wrong, and it does so unflinchingly. Polygamy. Rape. Sexual violence. Idolatry. (Never think that idolatry has nothing to do with sex.)

If sex is real, we need to call it what it is when sex strains against the very nature of reality — when it denies who God is and tells lies about what it means to be human.

The New Testament calls such sex *porneia*.

In English versions of the New Testament, the Greek *porneia* is often translated "fornication" or "sexual immorality." These translations may have lost their ability to convey the biblical idea of *porneia*, which is any kind of sex that violates God's reality. The word *porneia* is an umbrella term — one under which a number of different situations fit — for sex gone wrong.

Porneia is sex deformed by sin. It is sex that is contrary to God's good intentions.

To begin to get a sense of what it means to do sex in ways that deny God's reality, we'll look at a few times the word *porneia* gets used by Jesus. Jesus' teaching about sex is in continuity with the Old Testament and with the people of Israel. He assumes that there is such a thing as good sex and bad sex.

When Jesus gives instruction about how to live as faithful

witnesses to the God who is faithful, he addresses a question about divorce. Jesus teaches, "Anyone who divorces his wife, except on the ground of unchastity, causes her to commit adultery" (Matt. 5:32). Here, *porneia* — or "unchastity" — constitutes grounds for divorce.

Porneia is to violate the faithfulness of the marriage covenant. It is to deny the reality that God has created one-flesh union between husband and wife. *Porneia* is to cheat. It is to break faith with one's spouse.

Porneia, here, certainly includes adultery, but the church has also interpreted it as incorporating other sins against faithfulness, where those sins contradict the reality of faithful, one-flesh union. I understand abuse as a kind of *porneia*. Like the one who commits adultery, anyone who would batter and bruise a husband or a wife sins against his or her body. The batterer, like the adulterer, denies the reality that the spouse is truly, faithfully, united to him or to her, and the batterer, like the adulterer, embodies a false image of what God intends faithfulness to look like in this world.

Porneia is sin against fidelity.

Jesus also uses the word *porneia* in the context of his response to an attack from some Pharisees. They've challenged Jesus about hand washing, and Jesus responds, "What comes out of the mouth proceeds from the heart, and this is what defiles. For out of the heart come evil intentions, murder, adultery, *fornication*, theft, false witness, slander. These are what defile a person, but to eat with unwashed hands does not defile" (Matt. 15:18 – 20; the word translated "fornication" here is Jesus' *porneia*).

If we think like Gnostics, it will be easy to misinterpret Jesus here, to suppose that he's saying that bodies don't matter. The truth is more complicated. It's not just half of us that matters. The whole person — body and soul, outside and inside, mouth and heart — matters to God. Jesus teaches us that the inside and the outside — the heart and sexual behavior — are integrally linked.

It's an offense to the logic of Gnostic dualism to connect the heart (or the inner life, or the immaterial) to the body, the outer life, to mouths and hands and thighs and genitals. But this is precisely the connection that Jesus makes. Put another way, the inside and the outside are one whole. The inside shapes the outside. And sinful hearts produce bad consequences in the life of the body. Those consequences include *porneia*.

Porneia is visible, bodily behavior produced by hearts captive to sin.

Paul, like Jesus, uses the word *porneia* to describe the behavior of those who are captive to sin. In 1 Corinthians, Paul addresses sexual sin in the congregation, and his response is theological. It's about who God is. "Do you not know that whoever is united to a prostitute becomes one body with her? For it is said, 'The two shall be one flesh.' But anyone united to the Lord becomes one spirit with him" (1 Cor. 6:16 – 17). Paul draws here, as Jesus did, on the creation narrative to invoke the theological reality of sex.

"Shun fornication!" (v. 18), says Paul.

Reject *porneia*. Turn your back on it. Run the other way.

Paul teaches that we are saved not by works, but by the grace of Jesus Christ, which he poured out for us in the cross and the resurrection. Our understanding of sex-gone-wrong can never be one of works-based righteousness, as though we could get sex right in order to get our relationships with God right.

We don't get sex right and then come to God. The order runs the other way. God the Father, because of what Christ has done, restores us to right relationship with him in the power of the Holy Spirit, and that same Spirit dwells in us, giving us power to bear faithful witness in the world to what Christ has done. Part of that bearing faithful witness is to follow Paul and shun *porneia*.

The glorious truth of the gospel is that salvation doesn't stop with our forgiveness. It moves on into our transformation. Paul sees sexual holiness as an obvious part of this transformation or sanctification. As we are made holy, made like God, we become visible testimonies to what God has done in our lives. Part of what this means is to "abstain from *porneia*" (1 Thess. 4:3). Paul goes on to teach about God's good intentions for his holy people:

> For this is the will of God, your sanctification: that you abstain from fornication; that each one of you know how to control your own body in holiness and honor, not with lustful passion, like the Gentiles who do not know God; that no one wrong or exploit a brother or sister in this matter, because the Lord is an avenger in all these things, just as we have already told you beforehand and solemnly warned you. For God did not call us to impurity but in holiness. Therefore whoever rejects this rejects not human authority but God, who also gives his Holy Spirit to you. (1 Thess. 4:3 – 8)

Porneia is sex that rejects the power and leading of the Holy Spirit. And *porneia* is sex that exploits.

In the word *porneia*, we can hear the same root as in the word *pornography*, and there is plenty of overlap between the biblical idea of *porneia* and the contemporary porn industry. Porn takes God's good gift of sex and twists it away from reality. It replaces real, good bodies with fake, airbrushed, plastic bodies, and it trains us to desire — not reality — but this falseness. Worse, porn takes sex out of the context of relationship and places it, instead, on the market.

Porneia is sex that is bought and sold.

Christian sexual ethics are strange in the twenty-first century, but they were strange in the first centuries too. An understanding of why Christians looked so strange in ancient Rome might help us to understand how and why we ought to look strange today. It will also help us to understand more about *porneia.*

Historian Kyle Harper traces the process by which Christian sexual morality replaced — or tried to replace — the sexual morality of the ancient Roman Empire. Harper shows that the way Christians think about sex has always been *profoundly countercultural.*

It's not that the Roman Empire didn't have any sexual ethics and Christians suddenly brought sexual ethics in. Every culture has a system of sexual ethics, ways of policing and legitimizing what kind of sex is good and what kind is bad. In ancient Rome, sexual morality was mostly about the goods of the state. It was also about protecting the manliness of men with power. The word *porneia* referred to prostitution. *Porneia* was about sex being for sale and about the unfortunate people, men and women, whose business it was to sell it.

There were two kinds of women in Rome: honorable and shameful. There were wives, whose bodies were protected, and prostitutes, whose bodies were available for anyone's use. If you were a woman in the honorable category, sexual morality meant making it absolutely clear that your babies belonged to your husband. So, girls (and they were girls — twelve was the legal age for marriage) were to be virgins when they married and avoid adultery or any appearance thereof after marriage.

Modesty was the ultimate female virtue because it indicated you were the kind of girl whose babies would be sure to belong to her husband. And modesty was policed. "Ancient women," Harper tells us, "lived every moment engaged in a high-stakes game of suspicious observation."[8] Husbands controlled wives' bodies, and wives were for having babies.

Rome needed those babies. In a world where no woman could think of childbirth without fear of death, it was a free woman's job to produce babies for the state. Rome needed citizens and soldiers.

If you were a free Roman man, sexual morality was more complicated. Nobody even imagined that you needed to be chaste, but you were expected to engage in moderation, to show that you were in control.

Even then, it was acknowledged that moderation wasn't very likely in the years between puberty and marriage. Male sexual morality also meant following rules that made it clear that you were the one in power. We sometimes have the mistaken idea that pagan Rome was tolerant of same-sex behavior, but this isn't exactly the case. Pagan Rome wasn't surprised — or even disappointed — when freeborn men wanted to use the bodies of slave boys. But for those free men, the social "code of manliness" they needed to follow was "severe and unforgiving,"[9] and it did not allow for sex between grown men of equal social status.

Everything I've just said about Roman sexual morality was true if you were a free person. But the whole system depended on the existence of people for whom it couldn't be true.

Slaves.

Harper shows how "the sex industry was integral to the moral economy of the classical world."[10] Slaves were everywhere, and that meant that free Roman men had pretty much constant access to sex. This was seen as a social good. It kept young men from going after the bodies of other men's wives. Sex was cheap. Harper tells us that "commodification of sex was carried out with all the ruthless efficiency of an industrial operation, the unfree body bearing the pressures of insatiable market demand.... The wealthy had slaves to serve their needs.... Prostitution was the poor man's piece of the slave system."[11]

Roman sexual morality was about class and gender. If you were privileged, morality meant women had to be chaste and men had to be those of unwavering power and control. If you weren't privileged, if you were a slave, Roman sexual morality — being honorable — wasn't even an option. If you weren't one of the lucky ones, then dishonor was your fate.

I think we live in a world in which bodies are turned into commodities just as relentlessly as they were in Rome. Certainly, sex is still for sale in obvious ways. Bodies are trafficked, bought and sold. The porn industry rakes in the dollars. But sex is also for sale in less obvious ways. There's a sense in which our whole culture asks us to be temple prostitutes. Our world wants to make our bodies about *porneia* — and the commodification that goes with that — instead of about the Lord.

I have a friend who left the faith and threw himself into a world of sex without commitments. One of the most heartbreaking things I heard from him was the judgment that "it's a market out there, and you have to compete."

The forces of consumer capitalism are happy about this. They want my friend to buy as many products as possible to help him compete.

The promise of free sex isn't so free after all.

One of the strangest things about Christian sexual ethics — if you were an ancient Roman — was the idea that we are all free. Our bodies aren't for the state anymore. Our bodies aren't for the big men with the power. They're not for the porn industry or the beauty industry. Our bodies are for the Lord. We're free to witness and to love. Free to marry or not marry, to have babies or to not have babies, because the future of the world depends on Jesus, not on the size of the Roman army.

There are many ways that sex goes wrong. Christians don't claim this to shame people or to try to police other people's bodies. Christians claim this to tell the truth about the world.

We want to tell the truth about sex that is bought and sold. It's bad sex. We want to tell the truth about what it means to cheat — to break fidelity — and about what it means to be controlled by hearts bound to sin and selfishness and to have sex selfishly, without regard for others. When sex exploits, we tell the truth. This is bad sex. This is *porneia*. Bad sex is naked and ashamed — it hides from the light of day. And bad sex preys on the nakedness of others. Sex is bad when men and women deny responsibility for their actions, and sex is bad when it denigrates men and when it denigrates women.

All of this is *porneia*. Sin gets its claws into sex. It takes what was good and makes it into *porneia*. Maybe we could talk about "pornication" as an update to the language of fornication. To talk about pornication would be to refer, explicitly, to the biblical concept of *porneia* and perhaps it would help us connect the commodification of sex with what Christians identify as bad sex.

Pornication is a consequence of sin, but God has better plans for us than pornication.

The body is not for *porneia* but for the Lord (1 Cor. 6:13). God redeems what we have forfeited. God makes the broken whole. God heals the sick and opens up to us — again — the good delights of the garden.

4

GOODNESS REDEEMED

IT'S A STORY OF SEXUAL DELIGHT, OF UNABASHED APPRECIA- tion for bodies, of ardent desire. And it's Scripture.

If we're looking for a story to help us think about the goodness of sex, we'll find none better than the Song of Solomon (also known as the Song of Songs, or just the Song) in the Old Testament. The delight of the lovers is enthusiastic. It is sensory — touched and heard and tasted and smelled and seen. It is physical and celebratory. It is human and divine.

"Let him kiss me with the kisses of his mouth!" cries one of the Song's lovers, "for your love is better than wine" (1:2). The words have already evoked both taste and touch. Now they turn to scent. "Your anointing oils are fragrant, your name is perfume poured out" (v. 3). In just a few verses, we have an outpouring of verbs that are full of motion and joy and urgency: "love," "make haste," "exult," "rejoice," "extol" (vv. 3–4).

And then the lover starts in with rich and physical metaphors, comparing the loved one to all sorts of things that seem odd to us today, but which clearly appreciate the physicality and the particularity of the loved one.

> I compare you, my love,
> to a mare among Pharaoh's chariots.

Your cheeks are comely with ornaments,
  your neck with strings of jewels. (Song 1:9 – 10)

Ah, you are beautiful, my love;
  ah, you are beautiful;
  your eyes are doves.
Ah, you are beautiful, my beloved,
  truly lovely. (Song 1:15 – 16)

What happens when a mare wanders among the stallions of Pharaoh's chariots? The stallions go crazy with desire.

The Song is a love story in which sex is good and bodies are good. Desire is explicit; "My inmost being yearned for him" (5:4). If you haven't read the Song lately — or ever — I encourage you to read it through and to appreciate the celebration of bodily, sexual delights that is there.

Not one of us is exempt from the effects of the fall. None of us is exempt from sin. None from broken sexuality. We've committed sexual sin, or we've been victims of sexual sin, or the permeating reality of sexual sin has crept into our consciousness, crippling the way we think about sex. Sexual sin is pervasive, and it goes right to the heart of what it means to be human. It cannot be ignored.

But sexual sin — sexuality that is broken and twisted — is not the end of the story.

Paul isn't afraid to name the reality of sin, but he is also confident that a new reality — a deeper, truer reality — is ours in Christ Jesus. Sin — including sexual sin — is a description of "what some of you *used to be*" (1 Cor. 6:11; Paul's words, my emphasis). Because we have been restored to right relationship with the Father through the blood of Christ, things are different now. Because we have been filled with the power of the Holy Spirit, a new reality is open to us.

Sin *used to be* our reality, but God has intervened: "But you were washed, you were sanctified, you were justified in the name of the Lord Jesus Christ and in the Spirit of our God" (1 Cor. 6:11). Our new reality is holiness. Our new reality is to thrive — to be happy and healthy and holy — to live a life that is real.

Christians can name the goodness of sex because God is good. God frees us for faithfulness. God frees us for healthy, happy, holy marriages blessed with the gift of good sex, and God frees us to live the good life in healthy, happy, holy singleness and chastity.

We can reclaim the goodness of desire, we can reclaim delight, and we can testify to what God has done by being sexual in ways that are mutual, that treasure difference, and that reflect God's own faithfulness.

The story of sexual delight that we find in the Song of Solomon is a story of goodness redeemed. The work of God, which began in creation, has not been wiped out by sin, and God is working among his people to bring healing and wholeness and delight.

In the opening chapters of Genesis, we saw sex as God's good creation, and we then saw sex distorted under the condition of sin. Biblical scholar Phyllis Trible illuminates the Song as an explicit redemption of the brokenness of Genesis chapters 2 and 3. In sin, the garden of delights was lost. In the Song, that garden is rediscovered and reclaimed in the love between the man and the woman:

> A garden locked is my sister, my bride,
> a garden locked, a fountain sealed.
> Your channel is an orchard of pomegranates
> with all choicest fruits,
> henna with nard,
> nard and saffron, calamus and cinnamon,

with all trees of frankincense,
myrrh and aloes,
　　with all chief spices —
a garden fountain, a well of living water,
　　and flowing streams from Lebanon.
Awake, O north wind,
　　and come, O south wind!
Blow upon my garden
　　that its fragrance may be wafted abroad.
Let my beloved come to his garden,
　　and eat its choicest fruits.

I come to my garden, my sister, my bride;
　　I gather my myrrh with my spice,
　　I eat my honeycomb with my honey,
　　I drink my wine with my milk.

Eat, friends, drink,
　　and be drunk with love. (Song 4:12 – 5:1)

Trible writes:

Using Genesis 2 – 3 as a key for understanding the Song of
Songs, we have participated in a symphony of love. Born
to mutuality and harmony, a man and a woman live in
a garden where nature and history unite to celebrate the
one flesh of sexuality. Naked without fear or shame (cf.
Gen. 2:25; 3:10), this couple treat each other with tender-
ness and respect. Neither escaping nor exploiting sex, they
embrace and enjoy it. Their love is truly bone of bone and
flesh of flesh, and this image of God male and female is
indeed very good (cf. Gen. 1:27, 31).[12]

In God's redeeming power, desire is reclaimed from the
fall. Instead of disordered desire — the desire that would put
the human beloved above God — we catch a glimpse of happy

delight in the loved one. What if that delight is free to be happy and secure because it happens in a context of friendship and mutuality? What if that delight is free, happy, and secure because the lovers no longer have to grasp after it, trying desperately to meet an unmet need? What if we're set free from such grasping by security in God, by resting in God's faithfulness to us in a way that relativizes human love and so sets that human love free from the economy of sin?

> His speech is most sweet,
>   and he is altogether desirable.
> This is my beloved and this is my friend,
>   O daughters of Jerusalem. (Song 5:16)

In God's redeeming power, we may enter into a garden of delights where sex is freely given and freely received, where there is no price on bodies because we know that the price has already been paid in full by Jesus Christ. Those who know that they have been "bought with a price" are set free to "glorify God in your body" (1 Cor. 6:20). When all is grace, we can rest in love — both human and divine.

In God's redeeming power, hearts that were captive to sin are loosed from their chains. In God's redeeming power, our very bodies become temples of God the Holy Spirit (1 Cor. 6:19), and God gifts us with the power to resist exploitation. God gives us the power to relinquish sex that would use the other for our own purposes and to delight in the spouse who is both "beloved" and "friend."

Scripture allows us to think about *porneia* — along with all sin — as something dead. In Colossians, we're commanded to put the old life "to death," and that old life explicitly includes *porneia* along with "impurity, passion, evil desire, and greed (which is idolatry)" (Col. 3:5). Pornication — along with all sin — has been put to death and, in the power of the Spirit, we begin to live a resurrected life. That life becomes visible in our bodies. Paul is full of confidence about this: "If the Spirit of him who raised Jesus from the dead dwells in you, he who raised Christ from the dead will give life to your mortal bodies also through his Spirit that dwells in you" (Rom. 8:11).

Pornication is dead, and the Spirit gives us new life in our very bodies.

The whole great logic of death and resurrection surely applies here. Resurrection power works transformation. Resurrection doesn't ignore the old thing—the thing that has died, as though Jesus could have just remained in the tomb as if his body didn't matter. Neither is resurrection just reanimation, as if the Jesus whom the disciples met—risen from the dead—weren't transformed. Resurrection picks up the old, dead thing and treasures what was good there. Resurrection changes the old dead thing, burning away whatever was dross (1 Cor. 3:12–13) and revealing God's good purposes for it.

Resurrection works by continuity. The Jesus who died on Friday is the same Jesus who is raised from the dead on Easter Sunday. He still eats fish, and he bears the scars of his crucifixion. The seed that was planted in the earth is the same individual and the same species as the plant that grows from it (1 Cor. 15). God kills all those things about bad sex that destroy human flourishing. God kills all those things about bad sex that tell lies about reality, which fail to testify to the God who is faithful. When God kills pornication, he raises it from the dead as desire redeemed. He raises it as sex that tells the truth about reality. Desire is God's good creation, and God will not let it go.

And resurrection works by transformation. The risen Lord is changed. Sometimes his disciples recognize him, and sometimes they don't. He is no longer mortal — someone who could be killed on a cross. He is now the first fruit (1 Cor. 15:20) among those whom God will resurrect from the dead. He is now glorious, immortal, imperishable (v. 54). And so it will be when God transforms pornication into holy, healthy, happy desire and delight.

God can and does take what was selfish and transform it into love that is *for* others — for the spouse, for God. God takes what the sinful heart would have used to glorify the self and transforms it for God's glory.

God can and does take what was shame and restores it to the unashamed nakedness that is possible in the safety of covenant marriage, the safety of desire that does not exploit. God can and does take what was hidden and brings it into the light, for marriage and the sex that is its gift are publicly acknowledged and are supported by the community that is the body of Christ.

God transforms the blame-shifting of pornication into a love that takes responsibility for its actions. God transforms pornication's distortion of maleness and femaleness and opens up a love that values men and values women. God opens up, in marriage, a space for male and female to partner in good work. God redeems dominion and fruitfulness.

The Song gives us a portrait of love and of good sex in which the lover is also a "friend" (5:16). The Song repeats a refrain of mutuality. "My beloved is mine and I am his" (2:16). "I am my beloved's and my beloved is mine" (6:3). Thus, the Song highlights "egalitarianism, mutuality, and reciprocity between the lovers." This is shown in echoing, in "the mutuality of actions and the statements in reversal of stereotypical gender conceptions."

It can only be the resurrected desire of the Song that allows Paul to teach that "the wife does not have authority over her own body, but the husband does; likewise the husband does not have authority over his own body, but the wife does" (1 Cor. 7:4).

Where pornication is dead and the goodness of sex is redeemed, God opens up a garden in which such extraordinary self-abandon and mutuality is possible and safe and full of joy.

When God kills pornication and raises up, from that dead thing, redeemed and good desire, God makes space for true fidelity. In the garden of delights, complete faithfulness between husband and wife testifies to God's complete faithfulness to us.

The words of the Song testify to a love that cannot be destroyed, that is faithful no matter what may come. "Set me as a seal upon your heart," says the lover:

> as a seal upon your arm;
> for love is strong as death,
>   passion fierce as the grave.
> Its flashes are flashes of fire,
>   a raging flame.
> Many waters cannot quench love,
>   neither can floods drown it.
> If one offered for love
>   all the wealth of one's house,
>   it would be utterly scorned. (Song 8:6 – 7)

When Anne Bradstreet wrote a poem about happy marriage, it's no wonder that she alluded to the Song:

> If ever two were one, then surely we.
> If ever man were loved by wife, then thee.
> If ever wife was happy in a man,
> Compare with me, ye women, if you can.
> I prize thy love more than whole mines of gold,
> Or all the riches that the East doth hold.
> My love is such that rivers cannot quench,
> Nor ought but love from thee give recompense.[15]

Bradstreet imagines her love as that of lovers in the Song. She sees, in her happy marriage, an instance of what God can do when *porneia* dies and God makes way for utter, unrelenting, covenant faithfulness.

People have often wondered what a love poem — and a frankly erotic one at that — is doing in the Bible. Christians have interpreted the love between the bride and the groom in the Song in two important ways. First, the Song has been read as about the love between Christ and the church — where Christ is the bridegroom and the church is the bride — or as about the love between the individual soul and God. Second, the Song has been read as about the love, including sexual love, of human marriages.

Ambrose, a fourth-century bishop, typifies the first approach. Commenting on the Song, he writes that, "Having embraced the Word of God, [the soul] desires him above every beauty; she loves him above every joy; she is delighted with him above every perfume; she wishes often to see, often to gaze, often to be drawn to him that she may follow."[16] Ambrose sees the passion of the Song as indicative of the passion we should have for God.

Walter Brueggemann, a contemporary biblical scholar, is an example of the second approach. Brueggemann writes that "the book is love poetry of an unrestrained, passionate kind in which the erotic interaction of a man and a woman are brought to daring and imaginative speech."[17] Here, the emphasis is on the humanity of the lovers.

Ambrose and Brueggemann are not just examples of these two approaches; they're also characteristic of their time periods. The ancient church was much more likely to read the Song as an allegory and to emphasize its spiritual import for thinking about our relationship with God. The church today is rather more likely to read the Song as a celebration of the goods of human sexual love.

With another biblical scholar, Ellen Davis, I'd like to suggest that we need both approaches to interpreting the Song. This text *is* about love between God and humans and it *is* about human sexual love. Davis points out that, if we relinquish either interpretation, there are serious losses.

When we see that the Song is about the love between God and us, we see "a truly happy story about God and Israel (or God and the church) in love.... If the Song has nothing to do with the story of God and Israel at all, then there is nowhere to turn to hear one partner say, 'I love you,' and the other answer right back, 'Yes, yes; I love you too.' For this is the only place in the Bible where there is a *dialogue* of love."[18] When we recognize that the Song is also about human love, we are able to receive the Song's "strong statement about love between man and woman enjoyed in full mutuality and equality of status."[19]

I'm convinced the Song teaches us both these things: God and humanity are meant to be happy together in love, and humans too are meant to share happy, holy, bodily relationships with one another. But there is something even more important to note here.

There is a connection between God's love for us and the love that — in healthy, happy, holy marriages — we humans are able to have for one another.

They aren't the same thing, of course. There will always, always, always be differences between God's love for his people and the love we experience in even the best of human relationships. God is God, after all, and we are not.

But Scripture asks us to take this imaginative leap. It asks us to connect God's unrelenting, fierce, and faithful love for his people to the kind of love we get a glimpse of in human marriages. This suggestion is woven through the Scriptures, from the story of Hosea to Paul's "mystery" in Ephesians to the marriage of the Lamb, and we needn't shy away from it. The early Christians did not.

5

RADICAL FAITHFULNESS

EUSEBIUS, WHOSE EARLY HISTORY OF THE CHURCH LETS US glimpse the first centuries of Christianity, tells the story of Potamiaena. She was a slave who refused the sexual advances of her owner:

> Endless the struggle that in defense of her chastity and virginity, which were beyond reproach, she maintained against lovers, for her beauty — of body as of mind — was in full flower. Endless her sufferings, till after tortures too horrible to describe ... she faced her end with noble courage — slowly, drop by drop, boiling pitch was poured over different parts of her body, from her toes to the crown of her head. Such was the battle won by this girl.[20]

You read that right. Potamiaena died, one of countless early Christian martyrs who chose to be faithful unto death rather than renounce the faith. And her resistance to sexual assault — framed as desire for chastity — was what got her turned in to the government as a Christian.

Agatha's story is similar. She wanted to devote her whole life to God, and so she refused a senator's many offers of marriage. He had her tortured — including, at least according to legend, having her breasts cut off. She is still celebrated as a virgin martyr.

Lucy was the daughter of a wealthy family, and she too made a vow of perpetual virginity, a vow that would free her from marriage and allow her to give her fortune to the poor. The man she was betrothed to denounced her as a Christian, and she was sentenced to forced prostitution. When God protected her from this fate, she was burned and then died in prison of terrible wounds.

We only have the barest outlines of their stories, and even there the details are in question, but what survives of the stories of Potamiaena, Agatha, and Lucy certainly refers to a real historical phenomenon: Christians devoting their virginity to the Lord, even to the point of death.

I wonder if it's possible for us to imagine why any woman would make the choices Lucy, Agatha, or Potamiaena made. We live in a time in which sex is considered by many to be a necessity for anyone who wants to live a happy and healthy human life. And we are part of a church that tends to elevate marriage as the epitome of the happy Christian life. Can we take the imaginative leap into the world that shaped these early sisters in the faith?

Why would anyone die rather than marry? Were these early Christians insane? Were they prudes or Gnostics? Can we imagine a more charitable take on their lives?

Women in the ancient world were not free to not marry. Potamiaena, Agatha, and Lucy embodied the possibility of a very different life from what the empire expected, especially for women. They wanted to live as though it were really possible for our whole lives — including our bodies — to be *for* the Lord.

And people noticed.

Eusebius tells us that Potamiaena's martyrdom was the catalyst for the conversion of Basilides, her executioner. Her complete devotion to the Lord — signified by her virginity — was a witness, one that God used to bring someone else to Christ. Radical faithfulness spoke powerfully.

The last chapter explored how God redeems sex and desire as his good creations, and I noted there that part of that redemption is to restore the possibility of *radical faithfulness*. It's this last piece of goodness being redeemed — the piece in which we are able, through the power of the Holy Spirit, to be faithful in the way that Jesus Christ is faithful — that a Christian theology of sex goes public.

Christians have always acknowledged two routes for embodying faithfulness in a way that the world can see. We've always had these two routes for publicly declaring — and displaying — that God is faithful. The first route is celibate singleness; the second is faithful marriage.

In both conditions, Christians testify, with their bodies, to the power of God.

Early Christians valued singleness and celibacy, at least in part, because the single life was a sign of radical devotion. The virgin's body was a testament to the power of God, a testament to the fact that it is possible to be faithful to Christ alone. Singleness is a classic Christian way of life. In celibate singleness, countless Christians have chosen to devote their whole lives — body and soul — to God and to God alone.

In our time, it's hard for us to understand why believers in the early centuries of the church elevated celibacy and virginity so much. Not only was the celibate body sign of unprecedented devotion, it was also the case that to choose celibacy was countercultural.

Historian Peter Brown explains how deeply singleness went against the cultural grain. In celebrating singleness, the "church had become, in effect, an institution possessed of the ethereal secret of perpetual self-reproduction.... [Celibate singleness] announced to the Roman world of the late second century that the church was a new form of public body, confident that it possessed its own means of securing a perpetual existence"

To remain single and chaste was to declare that God was your everything, so much so that you had no need of marriage and children to secure your place in society or your legacy after you died. God, and not the empire, was the meaning of life. Service in the kingdom of heaven, and not family or country, was the measure of a life well lived. Conversion through Jesus Christ, and not birthing babies, was the way to everlasting life. Holy virgins, then, were a powerful testament to what God could do.

This is strange to us. It is strange both to the culture at large and to various Christian subcultures. That broader culture assumes that people need to have sex to be happy, to be fulfilled, and to live a full and flourishing human life. Christianity, especially Protestant Christianity, has reversed the early church's celebration of celibacy. Many Christians now act as though marriage — and with it sex — represents the fullest life possible. I frequently hear Christians equate maturity with marriage.

Given that Jesus wasn't married, this is a theological disaster.

Sex is good, but sex is not everything. Sex is good, but sex cannot be idolized. Sex is good, but sex is not God.

There's no doubt that our contemporary church does a bad job of valuing and supporting the single life. Single adults are subject to suspicion or are constantly asked about when they will marry or are segregated from the rest of the body of Christ in singles groups meant to get them *un*single. Maybe we've bought into the distorted cultural belief that there's something wrong with people who aren't having sex. We're in desperate need of reclaiming a positive vision of singleness.

Todd Billings, a contemporary theologian, finds resources for a positive vision of singleness in the Christian tradition. Billings draws on the ancient theologian Gregory of Nyssa, who gives us a vision of "the virginal body" as "productive and fruitful" and of the chaste, single life as "one of fullness and presence rather than absence."[22] Billings continues:

> Our great attachment, our great identity-shaping love, should be for God.... Gregory calls attention to the "freedom of virginity." The virginal soul, its attachments rooted in God, has freedom from "greed, anger, hatred, the desire for empty fame and all such things." Since the virginal soul does not seek after these other loves, it is not a slave to them.... For Gregory, virginity is not a curse or an accident, but a "gift" with great "grandeur." It does not result from God's failing to provide someone to love, but from "grace." The virgin anticipates the time when there will be "no distance between himself and the presence of God." ... For the Christian, virginity is not about loneliness. Indeed, for the Christian, it is impossible to be a virgin alone.... In a culture where sex itself is often enthroned as the ultimate saving, healing experience of presence, Christian virgins embody a refusal to make sex the ultimate consummation. Precisely because they are sexual beings, Christian virgins demonstrate that even unfulfilled sexual desires point to another ultimate desire: the desire for God.[23]

How can we envision the single life as one of unfettered devotion to God? How can all Christians — single and married — support one another as one family united in the body of Christ? Billings, through Nyssa, wants to embody chaste singleness as a full life and a fruitful life and as a life lived in community. Nyssa and Billings — along with Agatha, Lucy, and Potamiaena — are reflecting on and asking God for the grace to embody the truth of Paul's teaching to the Corinthians.

Paul's famous advice is for "the unmarried and the widows" to stay unmarried, like him (1 Cor. 7:8). Paul expects all of us who are in Christ to live with an urgency born of our faith that the kingdom is coming, that Christ will return, and that a desperate world is longing for the gospel. In this way, Paul expects us all to be in a kind of crisis mode, never allowing the church to grow complacent or to settle for the way things are.

We're to have sex — and not have sex — as those who are standing at the very gates of the kingdom. This is the gospel urgency that informs the advice that, "in view of the impending crisis, it is well for you to remain as you are. Are you bound to a wife? Do not seek to be free. Are you free from a wife? Do not seek a wife" (1 Cor. 7:26 – 27). Paul speaks with eschatological determination. The kingdom is coming. The "time has grown short" (v. 29).

Paul argues that the single condition frees people up for kingdom work. He's no Gnostic; he teaches that marriage is "not sin" (v. 28), but he would like his sisters and brothers to weigh the kingdom advantages of the single life:

> I want you to be free from anxieties. The unmarried man is anxious about the affairs of the Lord, how to please the Lord; but the married man is anxious about the affairs of the world, how to please his wife, and his interests are divided. And the unmarried woman and the virgin are anxious about the affairs of the Lord, so that they may be holy in body and spirit; but the married woman is anxious about the affairs of the world, how to please her husband. I say this for your own benefit, not to put any restraint upon you, but to promote good order and unhindered devotion to the Lord. (1 Cor. 7:32 – 35)

Like singleness, Christian marriage can also be understood as a public witness. Like chaste singleness, committed marriage is a sign of the divine possibility of faithfulness. As singleness testifies to the faithfulness of God, so does marriage.

The vast Christian theological tradition has always insisted that both marriage and singleness are good ways of life, good states of being, but there have been aberrations in that tradition. There have been instances where the church has failed to affirm that both marriage and singleness are good. In the early centuries of the church, there was a temptation to deny the goodness of marriage, and sometimes Christians elevated singleness and virginity to a status above that of marriage, but this was — and is — a mistake, and careful reading of Scripture and thinking theologically have always corrected the church back to affirming that both marriage and singleness are good.

After the Protestant Reformation, the opposite temptation became real. The Protestant reformers objected to the requirement that Roman Catholic priests be celibate; and those Protestant reformers tried to elevate marriage as they reacted against a perceived tendency to treat single Christians — especially the celibate monks and nuns — as super Christians. Against this, those reformers taught the "priesthood of all believers," a concept drawn especially from the New Testament book of 1 Peter. All Christians, those reformers insisted, are real Christians. All Christians, married and single, have status before God and may come before God.

Martin Luther, a former monk, shocked the world when he married Katie, a former nun. Their marriage seems to have been one full of love and affection and work for the kingdom of God, but it was also a symbol. The Luthers said to the world that married people — people who have sex — could be Christian teachers and leaders. There's a sense, though, in which Protestant elevation of marriage succeeded too well. The church bought the idea that marriage is a good so thoroughly that we forgot the many goods of singleness.

A good theology of sex needs to reclaim and proclaim the good of both marriage and singleness. In both marriage and singleness, Christian bodies are testimony to the faithfulness of God.

This is why Christian faith teaches that sex is for marriage. Why, if two people love one another, shouldn't they go ahead and have sex, married or no? The answer is that only married sex can testify — publically and radically — to the way God is faithful to his people. To have sex only in marriage is a radical sort of faithfulness, one that excludes premarital and extramarital sex along with adultery. The expectation that sex belongs within marriage and that marriage is an unbreakable union is the steady teaching of Scripture.

The exclusivity and unbreakability of the marriage bond is promised in the public vows that make a marriage. Traditional wedding vows are vows of radical faithfulness. In these beautiful words, wife and husband promise to be faithful, come what may. Having already testified to their willingness to "forsake all others," they promise to "have" and "hold" one another, "from this day forward, for better for worse, for richer for poorer, in sickness and in health, to love and to cherish, until we are parted by death."

Genesis implies that God's good, creative intention is for marriage to be like this — exclusive and unbreakable. This is what it means that the married "man leaves his father and his mother and clings to his wife, and they become one flesh" (Gen. 2:24). Exclusivity is seen in the "leaving" and unbreakability in the "clinging" and in the reality of the one-flesh union that married sex creates.

Exclusive unbreakability is also the teaching of Proverbs,

when men are counseled to be faithful to the wives of their youth and so to keep sex within the confines of marriage.

> Drink water from your own cistern,
> flowing water from your own well.
> Should your springs be scattered abroad,
> streams of water in the streets?
> Let them be for yourself alone,
> and not for sharing with strangers.
> Let your fountain be blessed,
> and rejoice in the wife of your youth,
> a lovely deer, a graceful doe.
> May her breasts satisfy you at all times;
> may you be intoxicated always by her love. (Prov. 5:15–19)

Here, in the poetic call for "springs" not to "be scattered abroad," we might hear an echo of the ancient Christian's desire that the celibate life be a way of resisting being scattered. Both faithful marriage and celibate singleness may, then, be ways of gathering up one's life and pouring that life, in one steady stream, out for God. Here in Proverbs, the expectation of marital exclusivity and unbreakability is that this comes with joy, with satisfaction, with lifelong "intoxication" with love.

Hosea's is a dramatic story of faithfulness, and it is explicitly a story in which marriage is a parable about God's faithfulness to us. God gives Hosea a surprising command, telling him to, "Go, take for yourself a wife of whoredom and have children of whoredom, for the land commits great whoredom by forsaking the LORD" (Hos. 1:2).

Hosea obeys, marrying a prostitute named Gomer, and Hosea remains faithful to her, even in the face of her unfaithfulness. In faithful marriage — exclusive, committed marriage — we have a powerful witness to the God of Hosea who promises:

> You will call me, "My husband," and no longer will you call

me, "My Baal." For I will remove the names of the Baals from her mouth, and they shall be mentioned by name no more. I will make for you a covenant on that day with the wild animals, the birds of the air, and the creeping things of the ground; and I will abolish the bow, the sword, and war from the land; and I will make you lie down in safety. And I will take you for my wife forever; I will take you for my wife in righteousness and in justice, in steadfast love, and in mercy. I will take you for my wife in faithfulness; and you shall know the Lord. (Hos. 2:16 – 20).

Here, we are the unfaithful ones and God is the faithful Lover. God promises to be faithful to us even though we fail, again and again. Even though we persist in sin and in idolatry. Faithful marriage is a sign of this faithful God and is possible by this God's power. Faithful marriage is a sign that God will bring us safely home, that God will destroy our worship of idols — those "Baals" who we've been tempted to chase after — and that God will be faithful in loving-kindness and mercy.

In the New Testament, Jesus and Paul both teach that marriage is meant to be exclusive and unbreakable, and it follows that sex is for marriage alone. We see this in the Sermon on the Mount, when Jesus intensifies the law against adultery and teaches "that everyone who looks at a woman with lust has already committed adultery with her in his heart" (Matt. 5:28). Here, Jesus reimagines faithfulness and takes it to new heights. Faithfulness involves both body and soul, both the inside and the outside of the human being, and marriage — and the physical and spiritual exclusivity that go with it — becomes an even more dramatic testimony to the God who is faithful.

As with Jesus, so with the teaching of Paul. Marriage should be the sort of faithful witness that cannot be broken apart. "To the married," says Paul, "I give this command — not I but the Lord — that the wife should not separate from her husband (but if she does separate, let her remain unmarried or else be reconciled to her husband), and that the husband should not divorce his wife" (1 Cor. 7:10–11). Here, we see Paul advising the Corinthian church in a way that is coherent with the reality that the one-flesh union of marriage should be a faithful, unbreakable witness. Even those married to unbelievers "should not divorce" (1 Cor. 7:12–13), if their unbelieving spouses are willing to stay.

Faithful witness is the reason Christian ethics have always held open two paths for Christian sexual fidelity. The path of faithful marriage is a sign of God's faithfulness. The path of celibate singleness is a sign of God's faithfulness. When a single person doesn't have sex, his body is a testament to God's utter refusal to forsake us. When a married person remains faithful, her body is a testament to the same God.

In marriage, we bear witness to the world to the quality of the divine-human relationship. As in a faithful marriage, God is faithful to us. The husband and wife who are faithful to one another, while being different from another, are a sign of the ways that God is faithful to us, while being different from us. Singleness is a sign equal to marriage as singleness too points to God's faithfulness. In both marriage and singleness, we're embodying something about God's radical fidelity.

Early Christianity was bold enough to imagine that all of us have — in Christ — the freedom to bear witness to who God is. The Christian understanding of sex was dramatic in the ways that it ran against Roman sexual morality. Roman women were not free to not marry. Christian women could choose — even insist on — celibacy. For Christians, women aren't property or baby makers. We're witnesses to the life of Jesus Christ in our bodies. Including in the ways we choose to have and not have sex. For Christians, men aren't lust machines or power mongers. They're witnesses to the life of Jesus Christ in their bodies, including in the ways they choose to have and not have sex.

In Rome, some people (potential wives, for instance) got protection and honor, and some did not. In the kingdom, everybody's body is honored. In Rome, bodies were for power or pleasure or the state or the market. In the kingdom, bodies are for the Lord. In Rome, sexual ethics were governed by different rules for men and women. In the kingdom, we are all called to be chaste, all of our bodies are not for *porneia* but for the Lord. In Rome, if you were sexually shameful, there was no going back. In God's kingdom, there is forgiveness and healing and grace and freedom.

Here's the kicker: in Rome, you were either a slave or you were free. In the kingdom of God, we're all free. As a witness to this, we value singleness and marriage as two routes, two ways of life, in which the Christian may be truly sexual and truly free.

6

FREE LOVE

N HER BOOK, *SEX AND THE SOUL*, DONNA FREITAS TELLS
Julia's story:

> "I didn't actually say no in the situation, but it just kind
> of happened," Julia says, recalling the first time she had
> sex. "I didn't really know that it had happened," she adds,
> explaining that she was confused about what having sex
> actually entailed.... "I actually called him later that night
> and was like, 'Hey ... did we have sex tonight?' and he was
> like, 'Yeah, we did.' And he was like, 'Are you angry?' And
> I was young, and I was like, 'No, no,' and at that point I
> had already made the mistake, so what was the point of
> stopping at that?"
>
> They didn't stop having sex. As Julia continues to
> describe her sexual experiences with this boy, I find myself
> struggling to think through what she has just told me.
>
> Julia was raped, though she doesn't see it as rape.

What happened to Julia is just one of many, many sad stories about sex that happens without consent. The problem of
sex-without-consent has surely existed for almost as long as sin
has existed, but it has also been compounded, and compounded
exponentially, by changes in expectations about dating that

started with the sexual revolution of the 1960s and escalated with the growth of the hook-up culture over the last few decades.

Sin isn't new, and coercion and sexual violence aren't new, but the problem of sex-without-consent draws our attention now because certain protections against it have been washed away. I am *not* claiming that we need to return to some earlier, pristine era, to a mythical time when people were generally more moral. I *am* suggesting that the chaotic situation of our present moment raises questions about consent in important ways.

What protections have been lost? They're simple things, really, and some of them were better than others: rules against closed doors, single-gender dorms, social expectations about how long dating couples would wait for sex.

We've also lost a lot of protections that were mostly about fear and shame — the "protection" that came with not having access to reliable birth control, the "protection" that came with fear of being ostracized for having sex — and I'm *not* advocating shame as a good means of changing our sexual behavior.

We don't need a sexual ethics based on fear. God, not shame, is the reason for chastity, and God, not shame, is the one who can change our behavior. I want to insist, as strongly as possible, that grace and the transforming power of the Holy Spirit are the only agents to make us truly chaste.

Still, a sexual culture based on "hook-ups" — sexual encounters that are supposed to be about pleasure only, that are supposed to come with no-strings-attached — is a sexual culture full of chaos. Especially if you're inexperienced, like Julia in the story above, it's very easy in that culture to end up in a situation where you're easy prey for sexual assault, for rape, and for any kind of sexual experience to which you don't have the chance to give strong and full consent.

Many have pointed out that so-called sexual freedom and hook-up culture demean women in special ways. This isn't a new insight; Augustine noticed the same thing centuries ago, when he wrote against the Manichean (a Gnostic-type group) teaching that procreation was a bad thing. Pointedly, Augustine accuses men who want sex without commitment, responsibility, and the possibility of children of turning women into whores. "Thy doctrine," Augustine accuses, "turns marriage into an adulterous connection, and the bed-chamber into a brothel." Hook-up culture assumes a horribly low view of what it means to be female. It reduces women to toys, to objects, to genitals, and fails to acknowledge the dignity of women as created in the image of God and intended for good work in the world.

There's a good argument to be made that our sexual climate also demeans men in special ways. Michael Kimmel has written about cultural pressures on young men to act according to the "guy code." That code is an unforgiving set of rules that young men punish each other for breaking. It prohibits showing emotions or any sign of "weakness," or a young man's masculinity will be questioned. The guy code and the rules of hook-up culture assume a remarkably low view of what it means to be male. It reduces men to animals, to genitals, to testosterone, and fails to acknowledge men as God's image bearers who have good work to do.

Hook-up culture obviously demeans relationships. It assumes an autonomous individualism that denies the interconnectedness of human beings. It steals — from sexual relationships — mutuality, intimacy, commitment, and faithfulness. In that context, real consent becomes illusive.

A sexual culture in which real consent is a problem is portrayed well in the web series the *Lizzie Bennet Diaries*, a contemporary rendition of *Pride and Prejudice*. Separated from Jane Austen by two hundred years and an ocean, by the women's movement and the sexual revolution, how might three postmodern suburban sisters live that story? Army officers become championship swimmers, a marriage proposal a job offer, and nineteenth-century British estate law a bad mortgage.

Elizabeth becomes Lizzie, a twenty-four-year-old grad student still living at home. As in Austen, Lizzie's charm is made visible in contrast to the unreal goodness of Jane and the dismissible silliness of Lydia.

It's hard to translate some of the bigger aspects of Austen's plot, and this reflects real distance between 1813 and 2013 in terms of sexual mores and the role of women. How to replicate the horror of Lydia running off with Wickham? It's very difficult to answer this question in a world in which sexual "autonomy" is such a given that it's almost impossible to call any sexual encounter a poor choice, much less imbue it with shame.

The solution, in the diaries, is to turn that elopement into a sex video, sold by a manipulative Wickham. An online countdown publicizes the time until Lydia will be fully exposed to the world. (As in Austen, Darcy will save the day, but it's an odd sort of saving when the whole Internet is already meant to know that the video exists. Exposure, not existence, is the problem.)

The diaries are doing the best translation they can in a world of incoherent sexual ethics. Lizzie's worries for the wild Lydia, long before the Wickham debacle, say a great deal about the absence of sexual ethics. In response to a "viewer question" about whether she is judging Lydia, Lizzie affirms what is surely cultural orthodoxy: "I'm not opposed to responsible, smart, safe women doing whatever they like in the bedroom with whomever they like…"

The next part of Lizzie's response, though, hints at trouble with this orthodoxy as a wistful Lizzie adds, "I just hope that Lydia *becomes* one of those women. Soon."

The ability to *meaningfully consent* is no given for Lydia.

How do we protect her? How can she protect herself?

One answer comes in the form of policies that try to bring the question of consent to the attention of the community and then try to define and require that consent.

An example comes from a policy instituted at Antioch College some time ago. That policy defined consent as "the act of willingly and verbally agreeing to engage in specific sexual conduct." It then offered an exacting set of "clarifying points," including:

- Consent is required each and every time there is sexual activity.
- All parties must have a clear and accurate understanding of the sexual activity.
- The person(s) who initiate(s) the sexual activity is responsible for asking for consent.
- The person(s) who are asked are responsible for verbally responding.
- Each new level of sexual activity requires consent.
- Body movements and nonverbal responses such as moans are not consent.[27]

While this policy *might* have been some use to Julia or to Lydia, the college was mocked in the media for its strangeness, for its draconian nature.[28] Certainly, there's something that isn't particularly human about it.

The problem of assault hasn't disappeared though, and mockery has now given way to very similar policies at many colleges. They may be legalistic and inhuman, but such policies provide some controls in an inhuman situation. Colleges, for legal reasons if none other, are trying to build some safety into the chaotic hook-up culture of contemporary campuses.

I don't oppose this. Protection is good. Safety — even relative safety — is good. Maybe this is the best some institutions can do, but it won't get us to real consent.

Only the Spirit will get us there.

What if consent is one of the most Christian things about the way Christians do — and don't — have sex? What if embodying consent in this world is one of the ways we can witness to who God is and to how God is faithful? And what if the traditional Christian expectation that sex be reserved for marriage is a way of safeguarding and treasuring the value of consent?

True consent requires mutuality. It requires freedom. That is, there can be no constraints on consent, nothing which forces or tries to force it. To consent is, from the Latin *consentire*, "to feel together."

This sort of freedom can happen only in marriage, because marriage provides a covenant context in which both spouses promise to be faithful even when trouble comes, even when we are vulnerable, even when we show our weaknesses and insecurities. Over the course of a long, healthy marriage, such freedom only grows.

Marriage ought to be that context which removes the constraints that would force false consent. Because marriage is that covenant context in which one should be loved, no matter what, there should be no reason, there, for sex unfreely given: sex given in the hopes of winning love or of keeping the other person around. There is no room, in the marriage context, for sex to be bought and sold.

Marriage, in a sinful world, is not always what it should be. I know — and grieve — that force, assault, and rape happen in marriages, but this is a distortion — an utter perversion — of what marriage ought to be. I also know that it is tempting to use sex as a bargaining chip in marriage and that sometimes people are even advised to use sex that way. This is antithetical to what marriage should be. The fact that marriage can be and is distorted does not undo God's good creative intention for marriage. Nor does it undo the possibility — the reality — that good, faithful marriages do happen in this world.

Marriage is that context in which consent should be possible in a strong, special way that exists in no other context. This is true because of the covenantal nature of marriage, but it is also true because marriage is a public institution, one that happens in the community of the church. This means that marriage is visible.

The marriage bed is rightly private. That privacy is part of the faithfulness — the exclusivity — that happens in marriage, and to make it public in certain senses would amount to a violation of faithfulness, a kind of adultery.

This is true, but it's also true that marriage is profoundly public. Part of what we do when we marry is to stand up before our friends, family, and church and say, "see this man? (or see this woman?) — I'm having sex with him tonight."

This making-sex-public builds into marriage a set of safeguards, a kind of accountability, which cannot exist in a private, individual agreement.

Marriage ought to be that context of truly free love — and truly consensual sex — in which we witness to the delight and freedom and faithfulness God wants for us in human relationships and the delight and freedom and faithfulness God shows in his relationship with us.

What if the strong version of consent that can happen only in marriage is a Christian witness against the commodification of sex?

There are endless ways in which sex can be turned into a commodity. Thongs and push-up bras are marketed to seven-year-old girls. The global trade in sex slaves is big business. Pornography so saturates the internet that stumbling upon it has become an inevitable part of the life cycle. Many become addicted to pornography. The advertising industry uses sex to sell almost everything: cars, beer, clothes, technology. All are marketed with the message that to buy the product is to get access to sex. Prostitution. Sex is used as currency in relationships, whenever one partner withholds or offers sex to get what she or he wants.

It's not a new thing, living in a world where sex is bought and sold.

We've already seen that sex as commodity was a pillar of the Roman Empire. Christian sexual ethics developed as a rebuke of that world. Christians claimed that Christ gives us the kind of freedom that allows us to choose sexual holiness. Truly consensual sex was a rarity in the world in which Christianity got its start. Christianity, we might say, invented consensual sex when it developed a sexual ethics that assumed that God empowers individuals with freedom, with what Harper calls "complete sexual agency."[29]

Christian marriage wasn't for the state, it was for God and for God's kingdom, and Christian wives weren't property, they were partners. Christians exercised their countercultural sexual agency by choosing lifetime virginity, and they exercised it by choosing faithful marriages. In their devoted bodies — single and married — they bore witness to the power of God and to the kind of free and faithful relationship God chooses to have with his people.

It's of great theological importance that Christian marriage is defined by consent. A public statement of consent is central to a Christian wedding.

> Will you have this man to be your husband; to live together in the covenant of marriage? Will you love him, comfort him, honor and keep him, in sickness and in

health; and, forsaking all others, be faithful to him as long
as you both shall live?

The Woman answers: I will.

The Man answers: I will.

In a world of tortured consent, there is a longing for a sexual
ethic that makes real sense. In a world — as in the *Lizzie Bennet
Diaries* above — where some creep may manipulate "consent" out
of one's baby sister, there is a need for a sexual ethic that gives
bodies meaning. The answer is not in some nostalgic call for a
return to Jane Austen's world, one in which women's sexuality was
surely as commodified as it is in an age of internet porn, but an
ethic that would give sex meaning in the larger story, an ethic that
would be coherent with personal identity and with the human
desire to live a life full of meaning.

7

THRIVING (AGAINST DESPERATE WAITING)

WHEN ELIZABETH SMART WAS FOURTEEN YEARS OLD, SHE was kidnapped from her home. Her kidnapper, in a sick and twisted parody of marriage, raped her repeatedly and called her his second wife. Smart's is a sad story, and it is one that probably captured the nation's attention for a lot of the wrong reasons, but she has used her experience to work as an advocate for victims of violence.

Smart was raised in a religious Mormon family, so she absorbed a set of teachings about sexual abstinence and purity similar to what many Christians are taught at home and in church. In her memoir, Smart makes a painful connection between the way she was taught about sexual ethics and her reaction to being raped.

Though she knew her family loved her, she had also connected her virginity — understood as her untouched body — to her worth as a human being. Despite her knowledge of her family's love, she recalls:

> A terrible idea seeped into my soul: If [my family] knew what the man had done to me, would they still want me? The question cut me to the core.... Imagine you have a beautiful crystal vase. Then imagine that you accidentally

knock it off the table and it shatters into pieces on the floor.
We all understand it isn't the vase's fault it was pushed off
the table and shattered. But still, it is broken. It is worth-
less.... That is how I felt. It wasn't my fault. But I was broken. No one would want me anymore. So even though I
knew the bearded man could kill me at any time, I had
already reached a point where I no longer cared.[30]

This is another tragedy on top of Smart's abduction and the
violence committed against her. Smart has been public about
how the feeling that she had been ruined made her less likely to
attempt escape from her captors. Those feelings make sense with
a certain way of thinking about sexual ethics, and unfortunately
that way of thinking has — too often — been substituted for gen-
uine Christian sexual ethics. But this set of teachings is false. It
is heretical.[31]

People are not crystal vases. Women and girls are not crystal
vases. People are not commodities. Women and girls are not commodities. Human beings and human bodies should never, never
be bought or sold.

Our value, our worth, our purpose in the world can never,
never be attached to some supposed purity of body, as if we were
merchandise instead of sons and daughters of the King.

If sex is in any way a sign of God's grace, it can never be commodified. It can never be wrenched out of the framework of free,
mutual, consensual relationship and placed on the market floor.

If sex is thus free, then sexual holiness cannot — cannot,
cannot — mean having a "valuable" kind of body or preserving
that "value" against loss of value.

But we've failed to be clear about that. Instead, we've bought
into a mistaken set of ideas about what purity looks like. We've

bought a set of rules that turn people into commodities and make sex into currency.

These rules are weeds that would choke the garden of delights that is ours in the Song of Solomon. Those weeds would strangle the glorious freedom of consensual, mutual, covenant relationship in which sex ought to happen. These rules are lies that convince us to prepare our bodies for sale to the highest bidder instead of delighting in our bodies and praying that God might use them as signs of the freedom of grace.

I'll call this set of rules the "purity paradigm." (I'm not opposed to purity, of course, but I am opposed to the false, market-driven version of purity that this paradigm sells.) In this paradigm, sexual purity turns the body into a commodity.

The purity paradigm understands purity as an attribute bodies possess, a physical thing that we can "have" and "lose." This turns bodies into commodities. Talk about purity is mostly talk about virgins, and purity for married people is not talked about at all. While responsible churches and sex-education curriculums may not teach this set of ideas as a whole, many people absorb the rules of the purity paradigm. They go something like this:

1. I can expect to get married as my reward for following the rules.

2. I need to grit my teeth and work hard to avoid sexual intercourse before my wedding night (to preserve the value of the merchandise).

3. This whole thing is probably more important for girls than for boys.

4. Possessing my physical virginity makes me pure.

These "rules" go profoundly wrong. They fail to recognize that sex is about who God is, which means that it's about the gospel story. The set of rules above is un-Christian. It subverts the gospel story and tells lies about who God is and who we, as men and women created in God's image, are supposed to be. Let's take a closer look at the purity paradigm.

What's wrong with believing that, "I can expect to get married as my reward for following the rules"?

The Christian life is not a life of following rules to earn rewards. The Christian life is a life of grace — full stop. It's a life full of beauty, and it's a life full of difficulties. It's always a life lived richly in the presence of God. We don't behave well in order to get God to give us a cookie or a cash advance or a spouse. As Christians, we confess that we can't — on our own — behave well. We are bound and broken by sin and stand in desperate need of grace at every moment for our salvation. When we are holy, it is not by our own power. Holiness comes by the power of the Holy Spirit who lives within us. If marriage were a prize given to winners of some purity competition, no human would marry. None of us is pure.

In the purity paradigm, the expectation that all Christians can expect a spouse also denies the beauty and the reality of the single life. It encourages us to think about purity as an adolescent concern, something young people will have to deal with for a few years, until they win the prize and get married. Here, the purity paradigm offers nothing to support celibate Christians after a certain age. It's turned into a concern for youth groups, and the church acts as though all normal adults will marry. This also fails to see that real purity — inasmuch as it is ours by the power of the Spirit — is a concern for the whole of the Christian life, from childhood through old age.

What's more, marriage is not a reward. Faithful marriage — like faithful singleness — is the way of the cross. Faithful marriage—like faithful singleness—requires us to die to self again and again, and faithful marriage—like faithful singleness—becomes a training ground for discipleship. In learning faithfulness to the spouse—a broken, annoying, limited human being—there is a lifetime of sacrifice, hard work, error, repentance, and forgiveness. Learning the limits of the spouse requires learning one's own limits too.

I'm not denying that marriage—like singleness—includes much that is rewarding, and certainly, in marriage, the delight of sex counts for a great deal in that regard. But marriage is not a merit badge nor is it a pleasure party. Marriage is a kingdom relationship meant for kingdom work.

This mistaken rule assumes that sexual holiness comes by human effort. It assumes that all people can expect and deserve eventually to marry and have sex. The "rule" also tends to be interpreted or practiced in a legalistic framework that either denies that people have sexual desire or allows for unmarried couples to push the boundaries of sexual intimacy very, very far as long as intercourse is avoided.

What's wrong with believing that "I need to grit my teeth and work very hard to avoid sexual intercourse before my wedding night (to preserve the value of the merchandise)"?

Your body is not merchandise. It's not a valuable item that will be "used up" or "spent" if you have sex. Having sex does not devalue a body. The bodies of married, sexually active people are every bit as "pure" as the bodies of virgins.

This teeth-gritting, desperate waiting also tends to create atrophied and legalistic definitions of what sex is. The purity paradigm turns sexual intercourse into the ultimate act that two human beings can engage in. This creates damaging cycles of behavior in which couples committed to "waiting" for marriage escalate physical intimacy in every way possible while avoiding actual intercourse.

The purity paradigm encourages an "everything but" pattern of intimacy in which couples push the limits of what it means to confine sex to marriage. People are able — even encouraged — to consider themselves pure when they're regularly getting naked with people to whom they are not bound in the consensual, faithful covenant of marriage.

Teeth-gritting, desperate waiting also repeats some of the mistakes attached to believing that marriage is every Christian's due reward. It turns chastity into an adolescent activity. It encourages us to think that we can will holiness, that we can work up purity and make it ours, by fiat. It thus encourages a works righteousness that's every bit as damaging to bodies and to souls as is the "everything but" version of purity just named.

What's wrong with the belief that, "This whole thing is probably more important for girls than for boys"?

Where do I start?

Not only does this belief make bodies out to be merchandise, it makes female bodies into merchandise in a special way. Male bodies, maybe, can be seen as human, as personal, as the tangible lives of human beings who bear the image of God, but female bodies are downgraded. Women and girls here are treated as property and our bodies are placed on the market.

This is, under the condition of sin, the way many — maybe, most — people and cultures have treated female bodies. They've been treated as property. As chattel. But God's good revelation to us in Scripture challenges this again and again.

Scripture insists that all humans are human, that all humans are created in the image of God. Scripture is explicit. When God creates humans in the divine image, "male and female" are included (Gen. 1:27). Scripture dignifies marriage, letting us see that marriage — and the sex that binds a marriage — is about mutual, personal, consensual, covenantal relationship. This is at least part of the meaning of the "one-flesh union" of Genesis.

Jesus returns us to that context in Genesis, and to God's good creative intentions for humans, when "some Pharisees" come "to test him," asking, "Is it lawful for a man to divorce his wife?" (Mark 10:2).

Behind their question, there was debate between Jewish interpreters of the law. That debate was about how to interpret a passage in Deuteronomy, which reads, "Suppose a man enters into marriage with a woman, but she does not please him because he finds something objectionable about her, and so he writes her a certificate of divorce, puts it in her hand, and sends her out of his house; she then leaves his house" (24:1).

The debate was about what constituted legitimate grounds for divorce. What could a wife do? What "something objectionable" would make it reasonable for her husband to divorce her? The rabbinic school of Hillel argued that Deuteronomy makes divorce legitimate if anything about a wife displeases her husband. The stricter school of Shummai taught that "something objectionable" could only mean sexual immorality and that divorce for other reasons was not permitted. So when the Pharisees bring their question to Jesus, they want to know if he sides with the permissive camp or the rigorist camp.

As he is wont to do, Jesus surprised them with his answer. He explains the passage in Deuteronomy, which seems to legitimize divorce, as a concession to our "hardness of heart" (Mark 10:5). Then he asks his hearers to think about God's good intentions for marriage: "From the beginning of creation, 'God made them male and female.' 'For this reason a man shall leave his father and mother and be joined to his wife, and the two shall become one flesh.' So they are no longer two, but one flesh. Therefore what God has joined together, let no one separate" (Mark 10:6 – 9).

See what Jesus did there? He refused to answer the question, refused to put himself in either the permissive or the rigorist camp. He reframes the conversation by making it clear that marriage isn't about getting a rule right. Marriage is about the big picture — about who God is and what God wants for us, and that big picture makes marriage meaningful.

Notice too that in refusing both camps, Jesus is more rigorous than the rigorists and far, far more full of grace than the permissive group. Where the rigorists would set the bar for dissolving a marriage high, Jesus teaches that one-flesh union of marriage is God's work and is not ours to undo. Where the permissive group would allow a man a way out of a hard marriage, leaving zero option for women, Jesus equalizes man and woman, binding both in a relationship that can only be possible by grace.

Jesus puts marriage in the context of discipleship. Marriage may be hard, costly. It may even be part of the gospel work of loving one's enemy. But Jesus isn't finished with teachings that would revolutionize the way his disciples think about sex and marriage.

He tells his disciples, "Whoever divorces his wife and marries another commits adultery against her; and if she divorces her husband and marries another, she commits adultery" (Mark 10:11 – 12).

This is revolutionary. People assumed adultery was a property crime, a crime against a man whose property (his woman) had been messed with.

People thought that men couldn't commit adultery. It was women's bodies that were property and so could be "stolen" or "damaged" by another.

Jesus — by making it clear that *men* can be adulterers — challenges the whole market economy that would buy and sell bodies, especially women's bodies. Adultery isn't a property crime. Adultery is a violation of God's intentions for humanity.

Jesus radically equalizes the man and the woman in the one-flesh union. Both are part of the mutual, consensual, covenantal freedom of that union. Neither may violate it. Neither's body is a piece of goods to be traded. Both bodies — united — should testify, in their union, to the faithfulness of God.

When we treat bodies as commodities, we deny Jesus. We deny the truth of his teaching here. We deny that human beings are — all of us — made in the image of God and precious children of the Father. We deny the nature of the one-flesh union, downgrading it into a cheap transaction.

And there's no doubt that we're far more likely to treat female bodies as commodities than we are male bodies. This sinful tendency is behind the assumption, in the purity paradigm, that the whole thing is more important for girls than for boys.

When we turn female bodies into commodities, we hurt girls and women. We also hurt boys and men.

If the female is a commodity, what is the male? Do we imagine him as a consumer?

Making the female into a commodity makes the male into a master, a strong man, a power broker. When we carefully protect female purity as a commodity, we often assume that male purity is an impossibility. We talk as though to be male is to be a monster, an uncontrollable lust machine who can't be expected to protect himself or others.

The purity paradigm denigrates men and women, boys and girls. It would make them — us — less than human beings, less than sons and daughters who bear the very image of the King, less than the sort of free beings who can and should enter into relationships that build others up, that are mutual, that are faithful and so point to the nature of the Father.

The purity paradigm turns physical virginity into a possession. This tendency heightens the sense that purity matters most for females and heightens the unbiblical idea that virginity and purity don't apply to men. The purity paradigm makes virginity into a thing that one needs to cling to in order to retain value. It tells the graceless lie that we are more valuable spouses for someone if we have this thing.[32] It tells the demonic lie that our market value is what makes us precious to God.

What if Christians taught that sexual holiness is not something we can achieve by our own desperate efforts? What if we taught that sexual holiness is a gift of grace?

One of the extraordinary features of Christian sexual ethics is that they are not just for women. Christian sexual ethics expect holiness and purity and chastity from men as well. Christianity was born in a world of stunning "indifference toward male chastity."[33] Jesus, that radical equalizer, expected chastity of all of us.

How might we do a better job, as the body of Christ, of teaching a faithful Christian vision of sex?

What if, instead of teaching that we can "expect to get married," we taught that everybody's body matters and that everybody's body can be a sign of faithfulness of God?

Instead of saying to children, "When you get married ...," we might say, "There are two ways Christians can live for God in this world, marriage and singleness." We might just say, "If you get married ..." instead of assuming that marriage is the default option for healthy human beings.

We might stop saying to single men and women, "When are

you going to settle down?" or "Seeing anyone special?" and say, instead, "I'm blessed by the way you live for God."

Marriage is a good thing. Sex is a good thing. But we have gone wrong if we suppose that marriage is the norm for being human, and we have gone wrong if we act as though we can't live meaningful lives if we don't have sex. We've also gone wrong if we treat marriage as a reward for good behavior.

What if we taught that men and women are precious? What could we do to make it clear that said preciousness is unconditional, that there is nothing we can do, nothing that can happen to us, that can take away our status as free, image-bearing children of the Creator?

How can we stop acting as if purity can be ours by an act of will, as though wise choices and self-control could make us pure? How can we make it known that the body of Christ is a body in which every member — male and female, single and married — is treasured?

Part of the answer to these questions is in teaching the gospel of grace. We need to repeat, again and again, the gospel truth that our relationship with God does not depend on us earning it. We are in relationship with God because of what Christ has done for all humanity in putting sin to death on the cross and in rising from the grave, triumphant over death. Our relationships with one another, including our sexual ones (perhaps, especially our sexual ones in that sex involves such complete and vulnerable mutual self-giving), ought to be testaments to grace. Sexual love cannot be conditional; it cannot depend on the partner meeting this or that condition. Sexual love cannot be purchased or coerced. If sex is to reflect something about the unconditional love the Creator has for us, if sex is to reflect something about the free grace of relationship with God, then it too needs to happen in freedom.

The marriage bed — a place of equality, mutuality, delight, covenant love, and consent — is the context for that kind of freedom.

8

BODIES BEAR WITNESS

SHE CAME TO TALK TO ME AFTER I'D GONE TO ONE OF THE dorms on campus for a conversation about sex and bodies. I don't remember much about what I said in the dorm — probably something about sex being a good gift from God — but I remember this young woman with perfect clarity.

She wanted to talk about the power of sexual desire, about how hard it is to be chaste. I gave her hope, she told me, because she'd never really met an "older person" who talked about sex as a good thing. She told me how she'd thought you had to be young — fit, svelte, airbrushed — to enjoy sex, because that's what you see in the movies. She thought she'd better hurry and enjoy sex while she's young, as there wouldn't be anything good left for the future.

To be frank, this conversation stunned me, but I think it revealed some deep cultural beliefs about what it means to have a body, what it means to look at other people's bodies, and what it means to enjoy embodiment, including sexuality. Our cultural orthodoxy makes bodies into idols, and it worships bodies — not all of them, but a privileged group of them. That worship ties back into the market idolatry I've been talking about in this book. The bodies that are offered to us as idols — the models, the sports stars, the gorgeous young actors — are, advertisers want to imply, bodies that we could buy. Pay for the youth serum, the fitness program, the protein powder, the designer clothes, and perhaps you too will have hope of being — or having sex with — the only kind of body that matters.

Christian faith rejects this idolatry.

Christian faith teaches that bodies are never to be worshiped. At the same time, it teaches that all bodies — including the bodies of those our world puts down — are very good. We can never worship sex or the body, and with that claim comes a freedom to value every body and to delight in the goodness of the bodily life, including sex. Even for — maybe, especially for — bodies that don't fit the mold of the idols on the screen.

Even, I wanted to tell that young woman in my office, for old married people.

Healthy, happy, holy sexuality — lived in married faithfulness and celibate singleness — is an emblem in this world of the relationship God has with his people. As God is faithful to us, our faithful bodies testify to his faithfulness. Our faithfulness is possible only by grace, only by the power of the Holy Spirit indwelling us. The faithful body is visible in the world as a testament to who God is and to what God can do.

Bodies can't be worshiped, and if we make the mistake of idolizing them, we get lost in the sad world where good sex is only available to those who can pay the market price. Only to the young. Only to the rich. Only to the powerful.

Bodies can't be worshiped, but bodies do matter. Bodies — sexual bodies — faithful in marriage and in singleness, are signs that point to the reality of God.

Poet John Donne wrote,

To our bodies turn we then, that so
    Weak men on love revealed may look;

Love's mysteries in souls do grow,
But yet the body is his book.[34]

"The body," Donne sings, is love's book. The faithful body can be a revelation of the God who is love. The faithful body tells a story of God whose love is steadfast, of God who desires his people, of God who reaches out to us, asking that we reach back in a real relationship of true mutuality. When we embody faithfulness — through fidelity in marriage and celibacy in singleness — we speak to a world in need of the God who is love.

When Paul, in 1 Corinthians, addresses questions about how Christians are supposed to have sex — and how we're not supposed to have sex — he goes straight to the larger question of meaning. We're back in the territory of reality here. What is most true, most real about God, about the world, and about us?

Paul is clear that we — as people who are in Christ — are "washed" and "sanctified" (1 Cor. 6:11). The meaning of our bodies rests in our relationship with the Father through Jesus in the Spirit. We are "members of Christ" (v. 15) and "temples of the Holy Spirit" (v. 19). These are giant, cosmic, theological claims. The promise of our future resurrection means that God gives us the grace now for our bodies to mean what they are supposed to mean.

God gives us grace for Jesus to be made visible in our flesh.

Do you not know that your bodies are members of Christ? Should I therefore take the members of Christ and make them members of a prostitute? Never! Do you not know that whoever is united to a prostitute becomes one body with her? For it is said, "The two shall be one flesh." But anyone united to the Lord becomes one spirit with him. Shun fornication! Every sin that a person commits is outside the body; but the fornicator sins against the body itself. Or do you not know that your body is a temple of the Holy Spirit within you, which you have from God, and that you are not your own? For you were bought with a price; therefore glorify God in your body. (1 Cor. 6:15 – 20)

Here, Paul insists that our bodies have meaning and purpose. Our flesh is for mission, for witness, for giving glory to the God who saves. And sex has something important to do with all this. In the way we have sex and don't have sex, we're supposed to be witnessing to who God is and what he has done. First Corinthians 6:13 is a focus verse here; "The body is meant not for fornication but for the Lord, and the Lord for the body."

Paul throws a wrench into pagan sexual morality when he makes it clear that good sex isn't about age or status. Good sex is about having our desire woven into the fabric of creation and redemption. Pagan Rome would not be surprised that "the wife does not have authority over her own body, but the husband does," as Paul says in 1 Corinthians 7:4, but it must have astounded pagan Rome to hear the rest of the verse: "likewise the husband does not have authority over his own body, but the wife does." The author of the Song of Solomon, though, wouldn't have been so surprised, for in the Song, Scripture gives us a portrait of sex as mutual, as delightful, as a reflection of the love God has for us.

Witness — in chaste singleness and in chaste marriage — does not depend on our perfection. Witness does not depend on our perfect pasts.

But in Christ we're free. And part of what that means is that we're free for our bodies to be "for the Lord." Our bodies — which are not for *porneia* but for the Lord — are finite goods. We don't need to be bought and sold, we don't need to join in the sex market, because we've already been bought with a price. Our bodies not our own.

We're finite. We can only take up so much space; we only have so many hours in a day. And even though we fight against those limits, they're a good thing. This physical finitude is the way we're created to glorify the Lord — within our limits. Christians have always seen that the work of glorifying the Lord in the body is work that can be done in two states: that of marriage or of singleness.

Too often we think of this as a hard either/or, but life is a lot less predictable than that. All of us are single for some portion of our lives. We may want very much to marry, but it may not happen. We may be married for years, but then find ourselves single again due to the death of a spouse. Within marriage, there are good reasons that couples sometimes can't have sex, after the birth of a baby, for instance. We can't always control whether we are married or single, but married or single, we are free to witness to the life of Jesus in our bodies by the way we do or don't have sex.

When — as single people — we don't have sex, we witness to the dignity and the purpose of the body. We witness to the fact that being human is not about selfish pleasure, being human is about glorifying God. We witness to the fact that there is more to life than easy indulgence. We witness to the faithfulness of a God who empowers us to be faithful in singleness. When we — as married people — have sex only with our spouse, we witness to the dignity and purpose of the body. Our embodied one-flesh union becomes a testimony to the faithful relationship between Christ and the church. In either case — marriage or singleness — all of our bodily finitude is for God. In either state, we're to embody the freedom that is ours in Christ.

Paul understood that marriage makes big claims on our bodies. He's not kidding when he says that married people have less time for other kingdom work than single people do. In 1 Corinthians 7, puts the body in eschatological space, reminding us — urgently! — that the "time has grown short" (v. 29), that unmarried men and women have a bigger share of their finite bodiliness to devote to the Lord than married people do. We all — married and single — do kingdom work. We all are meant to witness to the life of Jesus with the finitude that we have. But in marriage and singleness, the ways we can use that finitude look different.

Here's a little example. When my husband was in college, he played intramural basketball several times a week. That was a wonderful way of organizing the finite good that is his body. I would argue that basketball is — or can be, at least — kingdom work. A witness to the delight of physicality, to the goods of community in playing with friends, to the health and happiness and holiness that God wants for us.

Now that he's married and a father of four, his wife and kids make some pretty serious claims on the finite good that is his body. There's less room for basketball, and now he only plays a pickup game every couple of weeks with guys from our church. Marriage and fathering are kingdom work too. They're goods. And certainly, as a married man, the good of sex probably makes up for some of the lost delight of basketball.

But there are gains and losses, whatever state we are in. There are lots of good things my husband can do with his body, lots of kinds of kingdom work, lots of ways he bears witness to the God who is faithful to his people. There's basketball and there's fathering. Marriage means less basketball and more fathering.

In single celibacy, one hundred percent of the body can be devoted to kingdom work — for me, that work includes research and writing, friendship and hymn singing, service to the church and baking. As a married person, I still hope that one hundred percent of my body can be devoted to the Lord, but Paul is right. Marriage claims a huge share of my kingdom work.

If you're single, don't wait around for your body to mean something, as if the real good of being embodied can only happen in the married life. There's kingdom work to be done, basketball to be played, art to be made, friendships to cultivate, and a big world full of people desperate for an embodied witness to Jesus Christ. Married or single, the body is one hundred percent for the Lord.

Christian sexuality is meant to be a witness to the God who is faithful to Israel and to us. Sex is not about desperately waiting until you get married, then finally having it all. Sex is a witness to what God has done in our lives, the God who says to Israel, "I will take you for my wife forever; I will take you for my wife in righteousness and in justice, in steadfast love, and in mercy. I will take you for my wife in faithfulness; and you shall know the Lord" (Hos. 2:19 – 20). Bodies are not commodities or throwaway sites for gratification but are, instead, temples of the Spirit (1 Cor. 6:19), meant for real good and real witness in the world. Sex — having it if you're married and not having it if you're single — is kingdom work. It's a witness to the God who frees us for faithfulness.

My hope is that we might move to a theology of the beautiful body, a theology of the sexual body, in which the body becomes — not an idol — but something like an icon.

In the theology of Eastern Orthodox Christianity, the images called icons balance on the precipice between restriction and affirmation. Icons aren't painted; they are "written." And they are written according to strict rules reflecting the doctrine of the Orthodox Church.

Iconography is a firmly restricted discipline. Icons can only show what God is up to in the world. They depict not the essence of God, but God's work for humanity in the material bodies of creation. In the icon, we find an aesthetics normed not by the market, but by the glory and beauty of God.

In the icon, the bodies of Jesus and the saints are portrayed in a careful, disciplined way meant to point us toward God. The body of the saint is identified as witness to the Creator. A great diversity of created bodies is shown to glorify God. The theology of the icon has to recognize that we can't see God directly, but it also takes the fact that God was made flesh in Jesus Christ seriously, and it supposes that the icon may become a physical means by which we may enter into the very presence of God.

Might our bodies work on analogy to the icon? Might we become, as sexual beings made in God's own image, witnesses to the reality of the Creator? As writing an icon involves fasting and prayer, might the process of faithfully living in the body, including sexual discipline, be understood as something like the writing of an icon?

We see some of the issues involved in thinking through a theology of the icon in the Protestant Reformer John Calvin. Calvin is willing, at least in some sense, to claim that this good, physical creation opens up possibilities for our knowledge of God. Calvin speaks of light and of darkness, of glimpses of God, of mirrors that reflect God to us. God, Calvin says, "daily discloses himself in the whole workmanship of the universe. As a consequence, men cannot open their eyes without being compelled to see him." What we know about God is linked to what we see.

All of this seems a solid basis for supposing that the model of body-as-icon might be a helpful way of thinking about how we witness to God in the world. In embodiment, the faithful human creature may allow us to see something of God.

And yet Calvin is deeply opposed to any use of images to portray the divine. Calvin makes the stakes clear; "Man's nature, so to speak, is a perpetual factory of idols".[36] Bodies-as-idols would not have surprised Calvin. He knows how very capable we are of rendering ourselves captive to lies.

Jean-Luc Marion describes the difference between idols and icons as a difference between how "each makes use of its visibility in its own way."[37] The idol is an idol because it is not transparent. Instead of directing us beyond itself, it captures us and leaves us there, stuck. Unlike the idol, the icon points us to something beyond itself; it "provokes" a vision. The icon asks us to look beyond it to see how it testifies to the truth about God.

Paul uses the word *eikon* — meaning "image, figure, or likeness" — to suggest the way we might become this kind of icon, might point beyond ourselves to God. The *eikon* of Jesus Christ is what the redeemed human being is to bear (1 Cor. 15:49). Paul offers a great hope when he pictures human beings "being transformed into the same *eikon*," the image of the Lord, "from one degree of glory to another" (2 Cor. 3:18).

From the beginning of the church, Christians sought to live out sexual ethics in a way that looks different from the world. Our bodies — when, by grace, we do the kingdom work of sexual faithfulness — witness to the reality of a God who loves and is faithful to his people.

The analogy requires us to also point out the ways that marriage is *not* like the divine-human relationship too, but Ephesians chapter 5 pushes us to go there — to name those similarities and differences. Christ's love for the church is mysteriously imaged in the one-flesh union of sex:

> Christ loved the church and gave himself up for her, in order to make her holy by cleansing her with the washing

of water by the word, so as to present the church to himself in splendor, without a spot or wrinkle or anything of the kind—yes, so that she may be holy and without blemish. In the same way, husbands should love their wives as they do their own bodies. He who loves his wife loves himself. For no one ever hates his own body, but he nourishes and tenderly cares for it, just as Christ does for the church, because we are members of his body. "For this reason a man will leave his father and mother and be joined to his wife, and the two will become one flesh." This is a great mystery, and I am applying it to Christ and the church. (Eph. 5:25 – 32)

Sex is like Christ's love for the church in that sex unites two—who are different—in one flesh. Sex is like Christ's love of the church in that it is self-giving, even ecstatic, and it gives profligate care and grace and fidelity to the beloved. Sex is unlike Christ's love for the church in that husbands are not Jesus. Husbands, like Christ, may give themselves up for their beloveds, but husbands do not cleanse their wives and make them holy. (That's a job for God and God alone. Just look at the rest of the book of Ephesians.)

So we're dealing here, as the text says, with a glorious "mystery." Faithful sex witnesses to who God is, but we are not God. Sex, marriage, family, desire—all of it—is relative. It testifies to God's future, in which the whole people of God, "prepared as a bride adorned for her husband" (Rev. 21:2), will be united, fully—finally—ecstatically—faithfully—mutually—to Christ. Faithful bodies are signs of what God is up to in the world, but faithful bodies are not the point of the story. Sex is a pointer to the end, but it is not an end in itself.

Sex as faithfulness is a huge part of what the Christian body-as-icon looks like. When we carry in the body the image of Christ, we are a living witness against the many ways that violence is done to the bodies of God's people. Through the indwelling power of the Holy Spirit, the body ought to become a true mirror of God, a witness to what has been done in Christ.

With eyes redeemed, we will be able to see each other rightly as icons of the Creator. We might be able to look at each and appreciate all the beauty that is there without using the other for our lusts, without stopping at the body of the other and making it into an idol.

The sexual orthodoxy of our fallen world wants to create a body that is something to be consumed. Christian sexuality recognizes that the body is meant to be a witness. Sex is a witness to what God does in our lives, a witness to the God who is faithful and keeps promises, the God who says to Israel, "I will take you for my wife forever; I will take you for my wife in righteousness and in justice, in steadfast love, and in mercy. I will take you for my wife in faithfulness; and you shall know the LORD" (Hos. 2:19 – 20).

ACKNOWLEDGMENTS

Thanks go to Gene Green, indefatigable instigator of this series, and to the team at Zondervan, including Madison Trammel and Bob Hudson. Thanks also go to my teaching assistant, Alyssa Williams, for her help with the footnotes, and to friends and colleagues who have been gracious in supporting the writing process, especially Lynn Cohick, Tiffany Kriner, Christina Bieber Lake, and Nicole Mazzarella. I also want to thank the many students with whom I've had the privilege of studying marriage, sex, and family in the Christian tradition.

The book is dedicated to my parents and in-laws, whose long marriages are a witness in this world that faithfulness is possible. I'm grateful for many other friends who have been similar witnesses to faithfulness in marriage and in singleness. Thanks most of all to my husband, Brian. No words can express what I've learned from him — and from our children: Gwen, Sam, Tess, and Zeke — about embodied faithfulness.

Portions of chapter three and chapter six appeared in earlier versions in the *Christian Century*, copyright © 2013 as "Crippling Fantasies" and "Jane Austen in California" reprinted by permission from the November 19 and May 29, 2013, issues of the *Christian Century*. Subscriptions: $59/yr. from PO Box 420235, Palm Coast FL 32142-0235; (800) 208-4097. http://www.christiancentury.org.

NOTES

1 John MacKay, *A Preface to Christian Theology* (New York: Macmillan, 1941), 27.

2 Margaret Atwood, *Oryx and Crake* (Toronto: McClelland and Stewart, 2003), 144.

3 Irenaeus, "New Heavens and New Earth," *Readings in Christian Theology*, eds. Peter C. Hodgson and Robert H. King (Minneapolis: Fortress, 1985), 323–25.

4 Peter Brown, *The Body and Society: Men, Women, and Sexual Renunciation in Early Christianity* (New York: Columbia University Press, 1988), 116. Brown, at the end of my quotation above, is quoting an ancient Gnostic source, Sophia of Jesus Christ.

5 Kurt Rudolph, *Gnosis: The Nature and History of Gnosticism* (Edinburgh: T&T Clark, 1984), 253.

6 Sarah Coakley, *God, Sexuality, and the Self: An Essay "On the Trinity"* (Cambridge: Cambridge University Press, 2013), 10.

7 Ibid., 11.

8 Kyle Harper, *From Shame to Sin: The Christian Transformation of Sexual Morality in Late Antiquity* (Cambridge, Mass.: Harvard University Press, 2013), 41.

9 Ibid., 37.

10 Ibid., 3.

11 Ibid., 49.

12 Phyllis Trible, *God and the Rhetoric of Sexuality* (Minneapolis: Fortress Press, 1978), 161.

13 Richard M. Davidson, *Flame of Yahweh: Sexuality in the Old Testament* (Peabody, Mass.: Hendrickson, 2007), 569.

14 Ibid., 570.

15 Anne Bradstreet, *The Complete Works of Anne Bradstreet*, eds. Joseph R. McElrath Jr. and Allen P. Robb (New York: Twayne Publishers, 1981), 180.

16 From Letter 79, "To Laymen," quoted in *Ancient Christian Commentary on Scripture: Old Testament IX, Proverbs, Ecclesiastes, Song of Solomon*, ed. J. Robert Wright (Wheaton, Ill.: InterVarsity Press, 2005), 292–93.

17 Walter Brueggemann, *An Introduction to the Old Testament: The Canon and Christian Imagination* (Louisville: Westminster John Knox Press, 2003), 324.

18 Ellen Davis, *Getting Involved with God* (Lanham, Md.: Rowan & Littlefield Publishers, 2001), 67.

19 Ibid., 68.

20 Eusebius, *The History of the Church*, trans. G. Williamson (New York: Penguin, 1991), 184–85.

21 Brown, *The Body and Society*, 120–21.

22 J. Todd Billings, "More than an Empty Bed: Meditations on Gregory of Nyssa's 'On Virginity,'" *Regeneration Quarterly* 8:2 (Winter 2002): http://www.jtoddbillings.com/pastor-as-theologian-library/empty-bed. I'm grateful to Wesley Hill, at the blog Spiritual Friendship, for pointing out the Billings essay. Hill's work, along with others at that blog, is an excellent resource for thinking about the healthy, happy, holy single life, http://spiritualfriendship.org.

23 Ibid.

24 Donna Freitas, *Sex and the Soul* (New York: Oxford University Press, 2008), 149.

25 Augustine, Contra Faustum 15.7; from *Nicene and Post-Nicene Fathers*, First Series, Vol. 4, ed. Philip Schaff; trans. Richard Stothert (Buffalo: Christian Literature Publishing Co., 1887), http://www.newadvent.org/fathers/140615.htm<mt>.CF 15.7, NPNF 4.216.

26 Michael Kimmel, *Guyland: The Perilous World Where Boys Become Men* (New York: HarperCollins, 2008), 7.

27 Robert Shibley, "Antioch's Infamous Sexual Assault Policy," *FIRE: Foundation for Individual Rights in Education* (June 15, 2007), http://www.thefire.org/antiochs-infamous-sexual-assault-policy/.

28 "'Ask First' at Antioch," *The New York Times*, October 11, 1993, http://www.nytimes.com/1993/10/11/opinion/ask-first-at-antioch.html.

29 Harper, *From Sin to Shame*, 4.

30 Elizabeth Smart, *My Story* (New York: St. Martin's Press, 2013), 47–49.

31 Specifically, it is Pelagian and legalistic. Pelagianism is the name Christians give to the heresy that supposes that humans can—and should—do what we need to do in order to be in right relationship with God. Legalism is the

heretical belief that we can earn our salvation through obedience to God and good works. In the false teaching about sexual ethics I'm critiquing here, Pelagianism and legalism assume we can and should make ourselves holy by means of sexual holiness and that this is what gives us value to God. Pelagianism and legalism obscure the gospel truth that salvation is by grace.

32 Of course there is much that is healthy and holy and happy about the situation in which both spouses can come to a marriage without prior sexual experience, but this is in no way about their value as marriage partners.

33 Harper, *From Shame to Sin,* 52.

34 John Donne, "The Ecstasy," *The Complete English Poems,* ed. A. J. Smith (New York: St. Martin's, 1971), 55.

35 John Calvin, *Institutes of the Christian Religion* 1.5.1.

36 Ibid. 1.11.8.

37 Jean-Luc Marion, *God without Being,* trans. Thomas A. Carlson (Chicago: University of Chicago Press, 1995), 9.

Also by Beth Felker Jones

Practicing Christian Doctrine: An Introduction to Thinking and
Living Theologically

God the Spirit: Introducing Pneumatology in Wesleyan and
Ecumenical Perspective

The Marks of His Wounds: Gender Politics and Bodily
Resurrection

Scalpel and the Cross
A Theology of Surgery

Gene L. Green

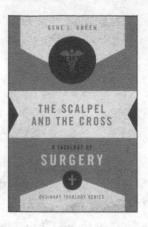

We know the bedrock themes upon which the Christian faith stands: creation, fall, redemption, restoration. As Christians, we live within these great moments of God's plan for humanity and all of his creation. In other words, our lives are part of Christian theology—every part of our lives, even surgery.

As a part of Zondervan's Ordinary Theology Series, *The Scalpel and the Cross* recounts New Testament professor Gene Green's encounter with open-heart surgery and carefully examines the many ways in which Christian doctrine spoke into the experience. The result is a short book that avoids shallow explanations and glib promises, instead guiding readers to a deeper understanding and an enduring hope in the face of one of modern life's necessary traumas.

Available in stores and online!

Political Disciple

A Theology of Public Life

Vincent Bacote
Gene L. Green, Series Editor

What might it mean for public and political life
to be understood as an important dimension
of following Jesus? As a part of Zondervan's
Ordinary Theology Series, Vincent E. Bacote's
The Political Disciple addresses this question
by considering not only whether Christians have (or need) permission to
engage the public square, but also what it means to reflect Christlikeness
in our public practice, as well as what to make of the typically slow rate
of social change and the tension between relative allegiance to a nation
and/or a political party and ultimate allegiance to Christ. Pastors, laypeo-
ple, and college students will find this concise volume a handy primer on
Christianity and public life.

Available in stores and online!

Cities of Tomorrow and the City to Come
A Theology of Urban Life

Noah J. Toly
Gene L. Green, Series Editor

Each day, the world's urban population swells by almost 200,000. With every passing week, more than a million people new to cities face unexpected realities and challenges of urban life. Just like the sheer volume of people in the city, these challenges can be staggering. As with the height and breadth of our metropolises, the wonders of urban life can be breathtaking. Like the city itself, the questions and challenges of urban life are both sprawling and pulsing with vitality..

As part of Zondervan's Ordinary Theology Series, this volume offers a series of Christian reflections on some of the most basic and universal challenges of 21st century urban life. It takes one important dimension of what it means to be human—that human beings are made to be for God, for others, and for creation—and asks, "What are the implications of who God made us to be for how we ought to live in our cities?"

This book is intended for Christians facing the riddle of urban creation care, discerning the shape of community life, struggling with the challenges of wealth and poverty, and wondering at the global influence of cities. It is meant for those whose lives and livelihoods are inextricably bound up in the flourishing of their neighborhood and also for those who live in the shadow of cities. Most of all, it is meant for those grappling with the relationship between the cities of tomorrow and the glorious city to come.

Available in stores and online!